HUMAN HISTORY
SOCIAL PROCESS

EAVANN MC CARTHY
Kerry Hendley. is a slapper

says
Eavan Casey
HUMAN HISTORY AND *so there!*
SOCIAL PROCESS

Johan Goudsblom
E.L. Jones
Stephen Mennell

Exeter Studies in History No. 26
University of Exeter Press

First published 1989 by the University of Exeter Press
© University of Exeter Press, 1989

ISBN 0 85989 332 4
ISSN 0260 8628

EXETER STUDIES IN HISTORY
General Editors   Jonathan Barry and Colin Jones

Editorial Committee
David Braund   Michael Duffy
Robert Higham   Malyn Newitt

University of Exeter Press
Reed Hall
Streatham Drive
Exeter EX4 4QR
England

Set in 11/12pt and 9/10pt Sabon

Typeset by Kestrel Data, Exeter
Printed and bound in England by Short Run Press Ltd, Exeter

CONTENTS

Introduction

Bringing the Very Long Term back in

Stephen Mennell

For many years, an interest in the long-term development of human society was faintly disreputable among both historians and sociologists. The very long term has, however, lately received distinctly new attention. This book is the outcome of collaboration between three authors—an economic historian and two sociologists, of whom one (myself) was originally trained as an economist—whose concern with long-term processes is of long standing.

Our common purpose is to explain the origins and development of major features of human society: priests and organised religion, military men, economic expansion and economic growth, and the puzzling counter-movements when long-term trends are reversed in 'decivilising' processes. These deep processes are each set in ecological and historical context. Together they contribute to an account of human history as an overlapping series of rationally explicable but unintended processes fundamental to the formation of modern society.

The book opens with Johan Goudsblom's restatement of the case for the study of long-term social processes in human history. Sociologists and historians have long been haunted by the ghost of Herbert Spencer and other Victorian social evolutionists who, in attempting to put their own society and its recent transformation in the perspective of the history of humanity as a whole, actually succeeded only in putting the whole history of humanity in the perspective of their own society. Goudsblom advocates a synthesis of chronology and 'phaseology' in a way which retains all the important questions posed by the old social evolutionists while avoiding the pitfalls into which their answers stumbled. Underlying the argument is a distinctive conception of the type of theory which sociologists and historians ought to be striving to construct: 'process theories'.[1] As Goudsblom writes, 'the processes come into the foreground, with "phases" or "stages" no longer defined as stationary states but in terms of the very processes of which they are a part and through which they are generated' (page 18 below). Traditional thinking in terms of a few causal 'variables' or 'factors' also rests on a reduction of processes to a sequence of static phases. That a similar quest for process theories underlies Eric Jones's thinking is evident when he writes of the search for prime movers in industrialisation:

> Models of growth usually assume the success of one or other novel force. The postwar experience of the Third World is however a graveyard of hopes that some particular propellant might be effective. Earlier British economic historiography is similarly a cemetery for an array of suggested push forces or positive shocks, none of them fully capable of accounting for growth in its industrial guise let alone as a general process. (Page 52 below.)

The meat in the sandwich of this book consists of two chapters by Jones and two by Goudsblom, having in common a principal focus on agrarian societies. That is to say, they are concerned with human society in the course of, and following, its second great ecological transformation—*second* because, as Goudsblom has shown in previous papers and a forthcoming book, the first and neglected great transformation was the domestication of fire. In chapters 4 and 5, he deals with the sociogenesis in agrarian societies of priests and warriors respectively. In an argument which avoids teleology, he shows how both of these great historic roles originated out of a compelling necessity for co-ordinated effort, which itself is a necessity in the achievement both of extensive and intensive growth.

Before Goudsblom's studies of priests and warriors we have placed Eric Jones's case for a very long-term and global economic history; economic growth provides the context for so many other long-term social processes. Jones's argument is in two sections. In Chapter 2, he urges that the *very* long-term historical record is of economic expansion, called *extensive* growth. In other words, economic output and total income were rising in pace with population growth. One implication is that there were continual investment decisions and continual positive economic activity. Although, over thousands of years before the present,

Introduction

Introduction

this aggregate growth was seldom strong enough to overtake the rise in population so as to produce rising average (as opposed to total) income, it had important consequences. Most significant is its role in the historical transitions (note the plural) to economic growth as it is normally understood: *intensive* growth, the rise of real income per head. These transitions Jones deals with in Chapter 3. *Intensive* growth did not burst suddenly and only once on a uniformly dreary world of stagnation, but emerged within the context of existing economic expansion. As Jones has argued in his earlier works, so-called 'modern' economic growth was not inherently as improbable as it is usually regarded. The technical and cultural barriers, though steep, were simply not as intractable as writings on economic development and much of the literature on economic history assumes. Once the process of *intensive* growth starts, it can overcome the worst of these difficulties relatively smoothly. The central difficulty lies elsewhere—Jones thinks in the realm of politics.

Essentially, Jones is starting with the simple, rather stark, behavioural assumption that—other things being equal—enough individuals in any large society will try to reduce their own material poverty. A largely unintended consequence of this impulse, as it is aggregated, is the expansion of the economy. Left to accumulate, there is no reason intrinsic to economic motivations why this expansion should not be sufficiently rapid to overtake the growth of population, thus producing *intensive* growth, rising incomes per head.

Why, then, does such a smooth transition not often work? The social process for our species may after all have been one of *extensive* growth rather than stagnation, but it has patently not been one of *intensive* growth since the beginning of human history. Yet one of Eric Jones's key observations is that there has been more than one transition from expansion to income growth. The trick is to explain the transitions. Here the argument is not that growth was positively caused, but that circumstances removed obstacles to it and permitted it to unfold. This thesis is methodologically convergent with Goudsblom's approach to the sociogenesis of priests and warriors. The forces which through-out most of history have operated to select *against* the common impulse to growth do, from time to time, weaken and move into reverse. If this reversal lasts long enough, the 'technical' or purely economic barriers will be overcome and a prolonged process of growth will set in. Usually this does not happen because a competing impulse is present: a compulsive tendency of elites towards rent-seeking, which amounts to using political means to capture the surplus produced by others, rather than directly 'economic' activities in the pursuit of wealth.

In Jones's view, the significant 'windows' through which a handful of societies has passed have themselves been the unintended results of fortunate stalemates when political elites have cancelled out each other's capacity fully to acquire the surplus, and may indeed have begun to compete with one another in offering services with which to retain relatively wide political support (Jones, 1989a). This probably characterises the European and Japanese cases.

A second route—'emergency marketisation'—is suggested by interesting work of S.R.H. Jones (1988) on the regime of Alfred the Great. An occasional government, instead of pursuing the customary route of squeezing wealth out of its subjects, frees factor markets and encourages commerce in the hope of thus providing revenues to meet a common foe. History offers, after all, multiple experiments, and every so often there appears a ruler such as Alfred. In Eric Jones's outline, the case of intensive growth which may turn out to fall into this second category of 'emergency marketisation' is that of Sung China, beset by the Tartar hordes.

In sum, the sequence as Jones envisages it involves the removal, by one of two mechanisms, of the forces commonly selecting against growth and certainly capable of restraining transitions to growth of the *intensive* variety.

One of Jones's major objectives is to provide a model which will at one and the same time encompass the earlier history of both the western and eastern growth poles so evident in the modern world. The history of *intensive* growth is not the same as the history of industrialisation, or of capitalism, or of democracy, or of the rise of the West. In the West, all these *were* interwoven in a spiral process. But once one has conceptually fused all of them together, it becomes difficult to extricate them. East Asia challenges this melding: the spiral there is not necessarily at all the same spiral as in the West.

Despite our different disciplinary affiliations, the three authors share a good deal of common ground. We share a scepticism about about the traditional economic history, heavily Eurocentric with its strong emphasis on an apparently unique sequence of events starting in Lancashire on 1 January 1760.

We also share a common attitude towards evidence and explanation. In particular we share a suspicion of all forms of mentalistic explanation, where culture, religion or ideologies are seen as the main engine of history. This may come across in what we have written as a hostility towards explanations derived from the work of Max Weber. Whether Weber himself can be blamed for the way his work has been used since his death is questionable. In his defence, it can be said that he was himself reacting against idealistic explanations in the German tradition, as well as against the vulgar 'Second International' Marxism of his time. As he remarked in the last paragraph of *The Protestant Ethic and the Spirit of Capitalism*, 'it is not my aim to substitute for a one-sided materialistic an equally one-sided spiritualistic causal interpretation of culture and of history' (1904–5: 183). Too often, the legacy of his work, especially in the anglophone academic world, has been to cause sociologists great excitement whenever they spy anything remotely resembling a Protestant Ethic, to be too willing—in our opinion—to acquiesce in idealistic, cultural explanations of differences in social development, and too ready to look for unique cultural ingredients in a supposedly unique European track of development. On the other hand, these faults are all avoided in one recent book, Randall Collins's admirable work on long-term developmental processes published under the title *Weberian Sociological Theory* (1986).

Weber and his generation did at least regard questions of long-term social development as central to history and sociology. In contrast, the three decades after the Second World War saw a 'retreat of sociologists into the present'.[2] This tendency may in part be the outcome of the sociological profession's wish to measure its achievements against the utilitarian yardstick of usefulness in rectifying the ills of contemporary society. It may also be in part a reflection of intellectual influences such as those of anthropology and of philosophers of science—Sir Karl Popper notable amongst them. In a book one purpose of which is to advocate the study of long-term processes, this deserves some comment.[3]

The rise within anthropology after the First World War of the approach known as 'functionalism', associated especially with Bronislaw Malinowski and A.R. Radcliffe-Brown, had a strong but markedly delayed impact on sociology. Functionalism involved studying societies as systems of well-meshing 'parts' at a given point in time.[4] It was at its peak in sociology during the two decades after the Second World War when Talcott Parsons—who had spent a year at the London School of Economics under Malinowski in the 1920s—dominated American sociology, and American sociology dominated the world. In anthropology, functionalism had begun as a methodological rule of thumb in field work: it was a reaction against the tendency of Victorian evolutionary anthropologists to resort to 'conjectural history' in seeking to explain the customs of preliterate societies, when for the most part any firm evidence about the past of such societies was lacking. Seeking synchronic relationships between patterns which could actually be observed in the field made better sense for anthropologists than hypothesising about origins in past time. Why the same ahistorical approach should have had such appeal to sociologists studying societies blessed with abundant written records of their own past development gives more pause for thought.

By the late 1960s, functionalism was in retreat in sociology across the world. The 'developmental agnosticism' (Wittfogel's phrase) it had helped sustain was then, however, strengthened once more through the influence of French structuralism on anthropologists and a minority of sociologists. Inspired by the shift in linguistics since Saussure from diachronic to synchronic investigations, Claude Lévi-Strauss sought the supposed eternal unchanging properties of the human mind underneath the surface flux and diversity. And in the hands of Lévi-Strauss and Roland Barthes, all history became myth.

Last of the culprits: Sir Karl Popper. Whether he had a powerful independent influence, or whether his views simply resonated with the currents just described, is an open question. At any rate, his books *The Open Society and its Enemies* (1945) and *The Poverty of Historicism* (1957) had, in Britain and perhaps elsewhere, a great impact on sociologists. Whatever may have been Popper's actual intention, my own generation of undergraduates in the mid-1960s somehow picked up the idea that it was academically and politically suspect to explain the present characteristics of society by any reference to the past.[5]

While sociologists and anthropologists were abandoning history, something similar was happening among historians. Historians, needless to say, could hardly abandon history. But there was a shortening of time spans. Perhaps it was increasing professionalisation of the discipline that propelled a retreat to the respectability of studies of short periods—at most, textbooks on one century or so, with a rare daring excursus to such stretches as the long sixteenth century (1500–1640).

Times have changed. Long-term social processes are once more under investigation by historians and social scientists. This is certainly not a single unified movement. Several new and unrelated tributaries seem to be flowing together, and the rediscovery of the past by social scientists and of the very long term by historians is at least as difficult to explain as the previous retreat. In part it is just a coincidence of key individuals.[6] They were often responding to a clear lack of historical context provided in recent work in their own very varied fields. Among sociologists, *Passages from Antiquity to Feudalism* and *Lineages of the Absolutist State* by the Marxist historian Perry Anderson (1974a, 1974b) were widely read, and so was Immanuel Wallerstein's *The Modern World-System* (1974). More recently, Hall (1985), Mann (1986) and Gellner (1988) have made forays into world history. Goudsblom and I, however, have for many years been working under the influence of someone whose at times lonely stand for a broad developmental sociology dates back half a century, and whose work has only received wider recognition in the 1970s and 1980s: Norbert Elias. His influence will be clear in our contributions to this book. All three of us have also long held in high esteem the work of William H. McNeill who, although honoured as a President of the American Historical Association for books of great historical sweep like *The Rise of the West* (1963), *Plagues and Peoples* (1976) and *The Pursuit of Power* (1982), remains to some extent a liminal figure who has said that his work is not yet regarded as quite respectable by the majority of his fellow historians. In the background too there has been the enormously influential work of the *Annales* school, the dominant voice for a generation and more among French historians. They, certainly, stressed the *longue durée*, although their work—inspiring as it is—in my opinion does relatively little to advance our *theoretical* understanding of long-term processes.[7]

Within the discipline of history, the rediscovery of the very long term may in part have been linked to the return of the survey course in undergraduate history teaching (Jones, 1985). In the 1980s, there was increasing recognition of the problems posed by the fragmentation of syllabuses, especially evident in the USA where a loss of nerve following the Vietnam War appears to have led to the abandonment of old-style

'Western Civilisation' courses. The volume edited by Josef W. Konvitz (1985) documents the debate about whether students should be taught resuscitated 'Western Civilisation' or newer 'World History' courses. Whatever the outcome, and especially in view of the deterioration of secondary education almost everywhere, it is not surprising that the need was first felt in lesser institutions where the calibre of students was such that they could not be trusted to have acquired or to 'get up' a standard acquaintance with the prevailing historical and cultural reference points. The need was less obvious at the Oxfords and Harvards—though in fact Oxford has recently instituted a comparative history course. The new world history movement is however far from merely undergraduate-centred, as is shown by the establishment of the new *Journal of World History* from 1990.

Within anthropology, there are also some signs of change. The controversial Marvin Harris has long pursued what he thinks of as a 'materialist' view, but which in our opinion would better be called an evolutionary and ecological perspective, implicitly developmental in its mode of explanation. More recent symptoms of a revival of evolutionary theory among anthropologists are the recent books by Hallpike (*The Principles of Social Evolution*, 1986) and Ingold (*Evolution and Social Life*, 1986). Ingold writes:

> By and large, recent anthropology has turned its back on evolution for all the wrong reasons. Of these, the most commonly cited is the one that equates the evolutionary paradigm with the establishment of a rank-order of societies that invariably places ourselves at the top. That is not, however, an essential aspect of the paradigm; what *is* essential to it is the idea that all human groups (ourselves included) are fellow passengers in the same overall movement, one that is irreversible and progressive, and hence that the differences between them must be relative to where they stand in it. But relativist anthropology, rejecting the notion of evolutionary progress and substituting the many worlds of culture for the one human world, in fact turned the imputed superiority of ourselves over others, observers over observed, into an *absolute* one. The enlightened few, liberated from the illusions of ethnocentrism with which all others were supposed to be afflicted as a condition of their belonging to one culture or another, could claim complete emancipation from the humdrum existence of ordinary people. (Ingold, 1986: xii–xiii)

The differences between the biological and social realms are such that we ourselves prefer to speak of 'social development', not social evolution.[8] Nevertheless, carefully used, ideas of adaptation and selection have a part to play in explaining social and economic development, as all our contributions to this book show. This, however, cuts little ice in the anthropological world, where the dominant voice is the intensely idealistic, relativist and *un*developmental 'symbolic' anthropology led especially by Clifford Geertz.[9]

Eric Jones's theoretical roots lie in economics. Of all the social sciences, economics is the most committed to explanations in terms of timeless, eternal laws of human motion, illustrated for the most part by reference to contemporary data. Jones, however, specialised for some years in the economic history of agriculture—and the pace of agricultural change through history is particularly conducive to taking the perspective of the *longue durée*. He describes his present theoretical position as 'a modified, ecological, economist's approach'. He shares some of the concerns of the 'New Institutional Economics' (see Basu *et al.*, 1987). One of its principal endeavours has been described as the 'endogenisation of institutions'; that is to say, the aim is to bring institutions—the structural organisation of societies—inside economic theories instead of leaving them outside as merely 'givens'. Of course, propositions about the structure of institutions have always been an essential component of economic theory. To give one simple example, Keynes's discussion of savings and investment involves propositions not only about rational choice (decisions to save and to invest) but also about institutional structure (that the two kinds of decisions are taken at any one time by two institutionally segregated categories of people). What economics has not done, on the whole, is to endogenise institutional *change*. My own concluding chapter uses my interest in 'de-civilising processes' as a vehicle for a further exploration of the complementarity of a sociology in the style of Elias and rational choice theory in the style of economics.

Finally, a little about the origins of this book. During Michaelmas Term 1988, the three of us jointly conducted a seminar on 'Very Long-Term Economic and Social Processes' at the University of Exeter. Johan Goudsblom had independently discovered Eric Jones's work through reading *The European Miracle* some years earlier. I eventually effected an introduction between the two of them, and then the opportunity arose for us to explore our common interests when

Goudsblom was appointed Visiting Professor of Sociology at Exeter, overlapping with one of Jones's periods on leave from La Trobe University as Professor of Economic History. Contributions to our seminar were also made by Eric Dunning of the University of Leicester and John H. Goldthorpe of Nuffield College, Oxford—both old friends of Goudsblom and myself, the latter especially invited as a committed Popperian to give an astringent scepticism to our proceedings. (Our guests' papers are not included in this book, since they were both destined for publication elsewhere (Dunning, 1988; Goldthorpe, 1988).) Our own chapters are the outcome of further discussion among ourselves and with members of the seminar; we should particularly like to thank Jonathan Barry, Stephen Fisher, Iain Hampsher-Monk, Michael Havinden, Helen Hintjens, Joe Melling, and Nadira Yakir. Goudsblom and Jones wrote their final versions in the early months of 1989; mine dates from July. A final coat of polish was applied by Eric Jones and myself when we met in Melbourne in August 1989.

Chapter One

Human History and Long-Term Social Processes: Towards a Synthesis of Chronology and 'Phaseology'

Johan Goudsblom

1. The Widening Range of 'Human History'

The terms in the title of this paper stem from two different, and diverging, traditions in European culture. First there is the idea of 'human history' in the sense of 'history of humanity'. This idea goes back as far as Classical Antiquity, where it culminated in St Augustine's bold attempt in *The City of God* to combine biblical history and pagan Roman history into one ecumenical history describing the vicissitudes of humanity from its earliest beginnings to the present.

The conception of an overarching human history has continued to inspire European writers well into the modern era. When viewed from a present-day vantage point, however, most of the works produced in this tradition appear to be hampered by some severe limitations. Instead of dealing with all of humanity they actually followed only one particular strand in the history of humankind; what they did was to put the Graeco-Roman and, ever since St Augustine, the Judaeo-Christian world into a historical perspective by following an itinerary starting in Mesopotamia and leading in time through Egypt, Palestine, Greece and Rome to Western Europe and North America (see Butterfield, 1981).

Our ability to see the limitations of this trajectory is of course not simply a personal achievement. It is due to the development of human society itself, and in particular to the enormous growth of readily available knowledge, enabling us to perceive things that remained completely beyond the grasp of Herodotus and St. Augustine, or even Voltaire and Gibbon. Our view, compared with theirs, has expanded greatly both in space and in time.

The expansion in space is obvious. As European writers in the sixteenth and seventeenth centuries came to realise, the inhabited world was larger than the familiar stretch from the Tigris to the Thames. Yet even for Immanuel Kant, writing toward the end of the eighteenth century, the word 'humanity' still expressed primarily an ethical ideal. He could not perceive it as the obvious—and in many ways menacing—reality which it has become for us today (cf. Elias, 1985: 71). Whether we like it or not, we are reminded of this reality the moment we open up a newspaper or turn on the television news. We all know that, for better or for worse, the citizens of Western Europe, the political leaders in Washington and Moscow, and the masses of the poor in Asia and Africa are mutually connected by far-reaching political, military and economic ties which—for all of us—strongly determine not only our present way of life but our very chances of survival. Global interdependency has become a hard and undeniable fact. Along with this, the need has arisen for a 'human history' that is not restricted to the old familiar trajectory but encompasses the whole world.[1]

At the same time that our idea of human history is expanding in space, it is undergoing an even more spectacular expansion in time. There is increasing evidence that the human past reaches back much further than could have been known until fairly recently. The 'classical' time perspective never went beyond a span in the order of seven to ten millennia. Even as late as the eighteenth century, the most enlightened minds had no empirical evidence of human records older than the Bible and Homer. They therefore could not possibly conceive of a human history or 'prehistory' extending back further than three hundred generations—whereas today every encyclopaedia tells us that the human past is to be measured not in hundreds but in tens of thousands of generations.

Not only can we now be certain that there are, and have been for many millennia, human groups living in virtually every part of the world, we also have some indication of the minimum time span of human habitation in different regions of the world. Thus we know that human (or hominid) groups were already living in the Americas more than 15,000 years ago, in Australia more than 40,000 years ago, in Europe more than 700,000 years ago, in Asia more than one and a half million years ago, and in Africa more than two and a half million years ago (cf. Wenke, 1984; *Past Worlds*, 1988).

Even if all the implications of this enormous expansion of the time horizon of human history are not immediately clear, it may well be considered an intellectual revolution.

2. The Primacy of Chronology in History

So much for the concept of 'human history'. Now, before I proceed to link it to the concept of 'long-term social processes' I would like to make one more remark about 'history' as such.

It is fair to say that history is a means for human groups to orient themselves to their past. Clearly, for this function, as for any form of intellectual orientation, some organising principle is necessary. The most important organising principle for history is chronology. Chronology, according to Webster's dictionary, is 'the science which treats of measuring time by regular divisions, and which assigns to events their proper dates'. It is, in other words, an intellectual device which helps us to arrange events in a uniform sequential order.

Now, such a sequential order is far from being self-evident, as all of us know from experience. We are all familiar with the difficulty of establishing, when recalling different events either out of our personal pasts or of a more public nature, which of these events came first, and, no less aggravating, how long was the interval between them. In order to cope with such problems we need, as Halbwachs (1950) showed, social benchmarks; these provide the chronology we need.

The oldest surviving attempt at constructing a chronology is the famous list of Sumerian kings (Jacobsen, 1939). This, and successive lists of ancient Assyrian, Babylonian, and Egyptian kings were drawn up originally for a use different from measuring time. Their immediate purpose appears to have been to establish the legitimacy of the ruling dynasty. The clerks who recorded the Sumerian lists did not shrink from measuring the reigns of the most ancient kings in tens of thousands of years; only as they approached the present did their estimates become more accurate and reliable.

As in the course of time the lists of kings gained in accuracy they also acquired a measure of 'autonomy' as instruments for charting the past. The struggle for a more 'objective' chronology, one that was less subject to the ideological interests of rulers, may still be witnessed in Greek and Roman historiography, for example in Thucydides' meticulous ordering by season of events in the Peloponnesian war. In the long run, the Olympic games in Greece, and the consulates in the Roman republic, came to serve as 'objective' time grids—generally accepted means of orientation in the past, relatively independent from the rulers' claims of legitimacy (see Bickerman, 1980). Still, using the names of monarchs as the markers for a chronology is a custom that persists unto the present day: we still refer to 'the reign of Victoria' or 'the coronation of Elizabeth II' in order to pinpoint events in time.

A characteristic feature of all chronologies (and I now deliberately use the plural) is that they tend to be *place-bound*. The list of kings of one country was not fit for another—as is still the case for us today: such concepts as 'Georgian' or 'Edwardian' do not apply to the European continent. In fact, all periodisations which are based on a chronological ordering of events—'Middle Ages' or 'Renaissance' no less than 'Tokugawa' or 'Meiji'—are equally place-bound. They represent attempts to characterise larger spans of time within a given chronological order that is confined in space. The continued existence of different religious calendars in the contemporary world testifies to the fact that a uniform chronology for human history at large is not something that is automatically 'given'.

3. Chronology and 'Phaseology'

I now come to the second term in the title of this paper, 'long-term processes'. This, as far as I know, is a comparatively new concept. Its origins, however, go back to a tradition that appears to be as ancient as the idea of 'history'—the tradition, that is, of conceiving the human past not in terms of the names and dates of individuals but in terms of impersonal stages or phases.

The idea that human society went through earlier stages before it reached its present condition was first recorded around the same time as the oldest lists of kings. The most familiar form this idea took was that of the image of a progressive deterioration of human life, from a golden age through a silver age to the present miserable iron age. The

Assyrians knew this wretched tale, and it emerged again both in the texts of ancient Judaism and in classical Greek literature (West, 1978: 172–77).

There is a marked contrast between, let us say, the book of *Numbers* with its long lists of lineages, enumerating every single father and eldest son on the one hand, and Hesiod's description of the descent from the golden to the iron age on the other. Both provide orientation to the past. In the former case this is done by means of specific names, in the latter case through an evocation of general characteristics.

To take another example, think again of Thucydides' great concern with chronology, and compare it with the way Plato and Aristotle wrote about what we would now call 'social evolution' or, perhaps more properly, 'social development'.[2] They too were referring to the past when it suited their argument, but it was a fictitious and undated past, called up only to make certain points about the present. Thus Plato began his discussion of the variety of political institutions in the third book of *The Laws* with a digression on the successive stages of shepherds, farmers and city dwellers—a digression which was very ingeniously composed but which lacked any claim to historical accuracy or veracity. The first book of Aristotle's *Politics* contains a similar passage sketching how first the family arose, then the village, and then the city. Here too the author did not bother about historical evidence. The model served only as a stepping-stone to his theory of contemporary society in which he found the family and the village to be (rightfully) subordinate to the city.

This indeed can be said about all models of stages current in classical antiquity: they were designed primarily to explain conditions in the author's present world, by showing how these had arisen out of previous conditions. The models hardly ever contained any dates or names. They were typological and indifferent to chronology and might be called 'achronous'. They all had a clearly evaluative tenor, as exhibited in the choice of the metals—gold, silver, and iron—to indicate the various phases. Most of the models also implied a sense of necessity. Whether the present state of affairs was decried as miserable as it was by Hesiod or appreciated positively as in Aristotle's teleological conception of the city state, it was invariably regarded as the climax in a series of stages.

Dealing with the past in terms of stages remained an element of European culture in medieval and modern times. It became a favourite intellectual device again in the nineteenth century for the leading sociological and anthropological theorists such as Comte, Spencer, Morgan, and Tylor (cf. Harris, 1968). They were all very much aware that the human past was far more extensive than conventional chronology could account for and they therefore sought to design new, general schemes of the social evolution of humanity at large. Unfortunately the available historical record was insufficient to permit them to fill in their grand schemes with empirical detail. As a result, the ironic situation arose that at a time when historians such as Ranke were becoming increasingly concerned with establishing the exact dates of events and with demarcating periods, some of their most brilliant counterparts in sociology and anthropology were taking a cavalier attitude towards chronological precision. What mattered to them was a theory of phases which might be used not only as a means of ordering the past but also for classifying contemporary societies and institutions. Their interest, we might say, lay not so much in chronology as in 'phaseology'.

The word 'phaseology'—which has been suggested to me by my colleague Abram de Swaan—may evoke derogatory associations. Theories of phases, as developed in the nineteenth century, have come under an avalanche of criticism in the twentieth. Many of the objections raised (for example by Popper, 1957, and Nisbet, 1969) pertain to the entire tradition of constructing phase models, from Plato and Aristotle to Marx and Spencer. Again and again, it has been remonstrated that the theories stemming from this tradition suffer from at least three serious defects: (1) they lack historic specificity and, consequently, testability; (2) they tend to mix factual and normative statements; (3) they imply a notion of inevitability and teleology. To these strictures may be added two others that have come very much to the fore in the last few decades: (4) they fail to explain the passage from one stage to the next, and (5) they are predicated upon the development of Western Europe and North America, and for this reason they are to be dismissed as 'Eurocentric'.

Against this total rejection of stage models I would argue that, as means of orientation, chronology and phaseology both have advantages as well as disadvantages. All a chronological sequence tells us is that one thing came *after* the other; a succession of phases has the advantage of suggesting other relationships as well, and it therefore offers the possibility of an explanation. Herein lie both the strength and the weakness of 'phaseology'; for the relationships which a model of stages suggests may sound very promising but on closer inspection prove to be either too vague to be testable or altogether spurious.

Another possible advantage of phase models is that they need not be inherently place-bound. Whereas each historical chronology was originally wedded to a specific dynastic or imperial centre, the postulated schemes of successive stages were formulated in a way that was as indifferent to place as it was to time, and this made them, at least in principle, ecumenical. The terms in which they were couched were intended to be applicable to humanity at large. But then, again, this very universality often made them unamenable to ready empirical testing.

The objections raised against the evaluative tenor and the notion of inevitability inherent in stage theories may be levelled against a great deal of nineteenth-century chronological historiography as well, concerned as it was with telling the stories of nations in terms of destiny and success. Nevertheless, these features of theories of social evolution were singled out for sharp criticism by such writers as Karl Popper and Robert Nisbet, who continued to recognise the spirit of Plato in virtually every attempt at discovering stages of social development.

What these critics have failed to acknowledge is that theories about social change themselves have changed, so that the objections levelled against Plato and Aristotle or even against Comte and Tylor need no longer pertain to them. One of the changes that has occurred is a shift in emphasis from 'phases' to 'processes'. This shift may also help to meet the objections that stage theories fail to explain the actual transition between stages and that they are implicitly 'Eurocentric'.

4. Stages within Processes: Elementary Sequential Models

The concept of 'processes' may serve as an elaboration on that of 'phases' or 'stages'. It refers to sequences of changes in the course of which something is transformed from one phase into the next. At first sight, there appears to be a fundamental difference between 'processes' and 'phases': the former seem to be dynamic—characterised by movement—whereas the latter seem to be static. At closer range, however, it is clear that processes of transformation seldom stop at a particular juncture; the normal course, certainly for social processes, is to continue in one form and direction or another, even when a new 'stage' has been reached. Every 'stage' or 'phase' is a passage in an ongoing movement; it consists of minor processes and it forms a part of larger processes.

Viewed in this light, 'process' turns out to be a more encompassing concept than 'stage' or 'phase'. This observation may lead to a reversal of the customary priorities in 'phaseology': the processes come into the foreground, with 'phases' or 'stages' no longer defined as stationary states but in terms of the very processes of which they are a part and through which they are generated.[3]

Stages or phases then, are continuing episodes in an ongoing process which are characterised by some relatively lasting features. Their boundaries in time are marked by specific transitions or 'turning-points'. In the context of human history, the turning-points of the most crucial significance are those which occur (1) when the process manifests itself for the very first time and (2) when (if ever) it reaches every known human society.

This may all sound highly abstract. Rather than continuing in this vein, let me give a few examples. As I have argued elsewhere, a major trend in human social evolution and history has been the increasing differentiation in way of life, and the concomitant shift in the balance of power, between human groups and all closely related animal species (Goudsblom, 1988). This process of differentiation has been going on for at least two million years. It has led to a gradually increasing dominance of human groups over all other mammals. As a result, inter-specific struggles between humans and other mammals have become increasingly less important for the course of human history (which is, of course, not to say that they have ceased to take place), while intra-specific struggles between human groups, especially groups organised as tribes or states, have become increasingly more important.

Within this overall trend some major 'catalysts' may be discerned— ecological transformations, brought about by human groups, that have considerably boosted the dominance of humans over other mammals. The first of these ecological transformations was the domestication of fire. Its initial effects may have been slight, partly because of the great costs it incurred. In the long run, however, the domestication of fire has been of enormous consequence, if only because it prepared the ground for the next two transformations with which most of us are more familiar: the transition to agriculture or 'agrarianisation' which began three to four hundred generations ago, and the large-scale application of fossil energy or 'industrialisation' which gained momentum only during the last ten generations.

Now, one of the interesting points to be made about these various 'sub-trends'—each of which is, of course, of momentous scope—is that they all constitute processes which are still going on. The emergence of agriculture did not put an end to the domestication of fire, nor did the industrial revolution put an end to agriculture. Humanity entered a new stage once certain groups began to live off cultivated plants and livestock, but it has continued to control fire and, more than that, to extend that control to an ever higher degree so that today temperatures of one million degrees centigrade can be produced. A conventional classification of societies into types marked by phases, say of 'agrarian' and 'industrial' societies, would fail to do justice to the fundamental fact that the processes which characterised an earlier phase usually continue to operate in the consecutive phase. They may become less dominant; but they do not come to a stop.

Clearly, this processual perspective does not exclude the possibility of distinguishing phases in social development. Thus, if we take as benchmarks the three major ecological transformations brought about by humanity, we may perceive four successive stages:

1. a stage when there were no societies with either control over fire, or agriculture, or mechanical industry, or x;

2. a stage when there were at least some societies with control over fire, but none with either agriculture or mechanical industry or x;

3. a stage when there were at least some societies with both control over fire and agriculture, but none with mechanical industry or x;

4. a stage when there were at least some societies with control over fire, with agriculture and with mechanical industry, but none with x.

This simple four-stage model may help us, first of all, to connect 'chronology' and 'phaseology'. Each of the turning points marking the transition from one stage to the next can, in principle, be located in time. Even if, at present, the actual dating may still be uncertain and controversial, the issue as such is clear and open to empirical tests. In addition, the model enables us to place the development of particular societies in the context of the social development of humanity at large. Classifying a particular society as 'foraging' or 'agrarian' is not enough; for an understanding of any specific foraging society we need to know first of all whether it was living in stage 1, 2 or 3—that is, whether it co-existed with agrarian and industrial societies. Finally, the model may remind us that we are dealing with continuing processes; one look at it may suffice to show that the rise of mechanical industry need not have been the last ecological transformation brought about by humanity. That is why I have added the *x*: we may well expect to enter or perhaps we have already entered a fifth stage, without yet being able to identify the latest transition as clearly as the preceding ones.

There is another set of propositions that may be inferred directly from the observation of the major ecological transformations. These propositions run along the following lines:

1. there was a time when there were only groups without control over fire;
2. then there was a time when there were both groups with and groups without fire;
3. we have now reached a time when there are only groups with fire.

These statements, implying a simple three-stage model, raise fascinating problems. How was the intermediate stage reached? When and where did this happen? How long did the intermediate stage last? Why did it end, and lead to phase 3, the climax stage?

With regard to control over fire, we have no empirical evidence about surviving groups representing phases 1 and 2; the discussion therefore has to remain somewhat hypothetical. With agriculture and mechanical industry we find ourselves on more solid ground, and there the same triad of propositions can be made: first, there was a phase in which no human groups had agriculture; then, one in which some groups did and others did not; and now, we have entered a phase in which every group has at least products of agriculture.

The same formulations can be made to apply to a variety of other institutions, such as writing, money, cities, or metallurgy. In each case the same sequential order can be observed, suggesting the same problems of when, where and how (or why) the intermediate stage was first reached, and of when, where and how it came to an end. In addition, our attention is drawn toward negative cases, where the intermediate stage did not lead to a climax stage in which the institution became universal; slavery could be an example.

5. The Interplay of Control and Dependency

By highlighting the three ecological transformations as major turning-points in socio-cultural evolution I do not mean to imply that they are to be considered as the the main 'determinants' or 'causes' of this evolution. They are best understood, I think, as catalysts which have triggered other processes, such as population growth and migrations, which in turn have influenced the ecological conditions with which people had to cope. In the configuration of all these continuously interlocking processes one general principle of socio-ecological dynamics seems to be of particular significance: the interplay of increases in control and dependency.

The three ecological transformations all constitute processes in which initially 'wild' natural forces are 'tamed' and 'domesticated', or, in other words, incorporated into human society. The 'taming' implies an increase in control: the natural forces are to a certain extent subordinated to human intentions. However, in contrast to what a superficial logic might lead us to expect, 'control' and 'dependency' are not opposites, and increased control does not automatically entail decreased dependence. On the contrary, by adjusting their way of life—including their pattern of reproduction—to a newly attained level of 'control' (over fire, over plants and animals, over fossil fuel) people make themselves increasingly dependent on that which they are controlling and on the apparatus by means of which they exert their control.

The principle of paired increases in control and dependency clearly applies to the domestication of fire. The control over fire enabled human groups to extend their food range and to enter new territories, and it made their lives in a number of ways more secure and comfortable. At the same time, however, as people grew accustomed to these advantages, it became increasingly difficult for them to do without them.

With the rise of agriculture the principle manifested itself even more compellingly. Increased control of crops led to increases in food and more often than not these resulted in increased numbers of people. In order to feed all these people, more food was needed. This led to the clearing of new land, which inevitably reduced the wild country available for gathering and hunting, so that people increasingly came to depend upon agriculture as their sole means of subsistence.

The interweaving of control and dependency—a relationship which is too subtle to be expressed in terms of one-sided causation—is a feature which may be observed in virtually all long-term social processes, and which may help to explain why these processes tend to move in a 'blind' and 'unplanned' way. In most cases the increases in control are likely to be the outcome of deliberate intentions, but the increases in dependency which they entail are just as likely to have been unintended and unplanned.

The principle of paired increases in control and dependency, with its implications for the blind course of social evolution, is a principle of far-reaching scope. It is not, however, a 'law' which could be expressed in a fixed formula. I would rather adapt Herbert Blumer's (1969: 140–52) term 'sensitising concept', and refer to this principle as a 'sensitising idea', directing our attention towards an important feature of very long-term social processes that can be observed in a great variety of empirical instances. I would even venture the hypothesis that it is a principle of such wide scope that, unless clear instances be found in which its presence cannot be demonstrated, it may be regarded as universal.

6. Dominant Trends

In dealing with long-term processes it seems useful to distinguish between universal and dominant trends. The trend towards specialisation, for example, may be universal, but then so may be the trend towards *de*specialisation, as a part of the tendency towards social entropy that seems to be present in every society. It may not be a bad rule of thumb and not an unsound research strategy to assume that for any given trend a counter-trend may be found, operating in the opposite direction. The principle of paired increases in control and dependency would support this assumptiom, and so would the consideration that changes which are beneficial to some people are almost bound to be harmful to others. Even if those others are small in numbers or weak in power, they are nevertheless likely to put up some resistance and this resistance then constitutes a countervailing tendency.

There would have been no socio-cultural evolution, however, if every trend had always been offset by equally strong counter-trends. The problem is, therefore, to identify the dominant trends and to seek how they may be explained.

One major trend in human history, to which I have already alluded, is the increasing differentiation between human groups and all other mammals. This trend has been dominant for at least two million years and it is still continuing. There can be no doubt that the long-established predominance of humans over other animals was a precondition for the emergence of agriculture around ten thousand years ago. But then, as so often happens with preconditions, this predominance was reinforced by the further development of farming.

Ever since then, over the past ten thousand years, a cluster of closely interrelated trends has been dominant in human history. They did not immediately prevail everywhere, but once set into motion in certain areas they tended to spread until, in the twentieth century, they have become dominant trends in all societies all over the world. Maybe some societies have now reached a stage in which some of these trends are beginning to be outweighed by countervailing movements. In the large majority of contemporary societies, however, these are still the dominant trends.

As a direct result of agriculture there was a trend towards higher production of food in increasingly more concentrated areas (from 'shifting cultivation' to 'multi-cropping'—see Boserup, 1965: 15–16) leading to an *increase in numbers* of the human population and to an increasing *concentration* of people in ever more densely populated areas. Both within and among these areas of dense settlement there were processes of *specialisation* as to social functions and of *organisation* in increasingly large units such as states, markets and religious cults. As specialisation and organisation proceeded, they gave rise to increasing differences in power, property and prestige, in other words to a process of social *stratification*.

In a way, these five trends represent variations on the theme of differentiation and integration which Herbert Spencer (1874) indicated as the twin motive forces underlying evolution in general. The growth, concentration and increasing organisation of human populations may be seen as reflecting integration, specialisation as reflecting differentiation, and organisation as reflecting both. In view of the close interrelations between the five trends it would seem futile to try to identify one of them as the 'prime mover'. It is more fruitful to chart the course which the trends have actually taken and then to seek an explanation for their overall dynamics, including oscillations, stagnations and regressions.

It is not difficult to think of various cases in which the trends never were dominant or ceased to be so. The 'decline and fall of the Roman empire' probably comes to mind first of all, but it is by no means the only counter-example (Tainter, 1988). However, even if the historical cases of stagnation and reversal prove to outnumber those in which the five trends did proceed, the remarkable fact remains that *in the long run* the dominant trends continued and left no society unaffected.

The 'long run' is crucial. Clearly no single society has continued to veer unwaveringly through the ages in the direction of the five trends. The trends have remained dominant, however, for humanity at large. Taking the calculations of Rein Taagepera (1978) about the size and duration of empires as a clue we could formulate the following hypotheses. Over the past ten millennia, in any random year (1) the total size of the human population and (2) the size of the then largest concentration of people on earth has been greater than either was 1,000 years before. Moreover, the highest degree of (3) specialisation, (4) organisation and (5) stratification to be found anywhere in the world was also greater than it was 1,000 years before. Perhaps, because we are still lacking sufficient empirical evidence and appropriate means of operationalisation, these hypotheses are too bold to be testable yet. They may help, nevertheless, to make us familiar with the idea that sensible propositions about very long-term processes can be made.

Once we are prepared to accept this idea there is no longer any reason to espouse what Karl Wittfogel (1957: 7) has aptly called 'developmental agnosticism'. Such agnosticism is quite rampant among historians and social scientists today. In order to overcome it we shall have to avoid conceiving of very long-term processes in mono-causal, teleological and normative terms. The fact that social evolution has gone on in a certain direction for many millennia does not imply that it is determined by any particular cause, nor that it is attuned to any particular purpose, nor that it corresponds to any particular ideal. In each of these respects agnosticism is called for, but this sceptical attitude need not affect the conception of long-term social processes and of social development as such.

The many diverse forms which human culture can take may easily blind us to the common pattern in the processes of social development. Part of this pattern may be due to general tendencies inherent in each and every society at a certain stage of development. In addition we shall always have to reckon with the possibility that any particular society may, because of its specific ecological and sociological conditions, initiate processes which then radiate into other, neighbouring societies and acquire a momentum of their own. Population growth may be a case in point. It did not take place always and everywhere, and certainly not at the same rate (cf. Harris and Ross, 1987). Even for humanity at large, growth probably did not proceed in an unbroken fashion: there were periods of stagnation and decline. In the long run the growth trend proved to be dominant, however, because societies which happened to develop high growth rates could not fail to influence those with low growth rates (and *vice versa*, it should be added.) Changing population pressures led to waves of migration—sometimes peaceful, more often violent—which tended to follow two contrary currents: one from the centres of urban settlement to the rural areas and the periphery, and one in the opposite direction. Many of the major events in the history of individual peoples and nations have taken place, as William McNeill (1984) shows, in the context of these far-reaching migration movements.

7. Human History and Sociology

As I pointed out at the beginning of this chapter, there are two reasons for some of us today to engage in the study of human history, in spite of its formidable scope. One is the topicality of the subject now that humanity's increasing global interdependence is so clearly manifest. The other is the growing insight that global interdependence is far less recent than we may have been led to believe. There never was a time when the history of any people could evolve for generations without it being affected by its neighbours—who were affected by *their* neighbours, and so on. Therefore, the history of humanity forms the all-encompassing framework in which all the events have taken place that form the subject matter of more particular histories. It goes without saying that our conception of human history must be compatible with all the known facts, but it should be equally obvious that all knowledge of facts relating to specific historical events remains somewhat loose and 'up in the air' if it cannot be connected with this larger framework. As McNeill (1986: 44) remarks, 'only by accepting and then acting on a theory of social process can historians expect to have a criterion of relevance to guide them amidst the confusing plethora of data potentially available to their researches'. Sociologists, on the other hand, as Michael Mann (1986: 173) notes, in drawing up their theoretical schemes and comparative models, 'must be restrained by an appreciation of world-historical time'. It is in the study of human history and long-term social processes that these desiderata can be jointly met: here historians attain their highest level of generality, while sociologists are confronted with the dictates of chronology. Here, more than anywhere else, it becomes evident that, in Norman Gottwald's words, 'history without sociology is blind, sociology without history is empty', (1979: 17).

History and sociology are so complementary at this level that ideally speaking they could merge completely. In actual practice the chances of this happening are very slight. This is largely due to the diverging group cultures which have developed historically and constitute an unavoidable social fact (cf. Burke, 1980). The very lack of a synthesis in the form of a common theory of human history and social evolution reflects the professional frictions which beset the working relationships between the two disciplines. At the same time, as so often in social and cultural processes, the 'effect' also operates as a 'cause': the lack of a common theory continues to keep historians and sociologists apart.

Still we should not give up our attempts to reach at least a common theoretical perspective. Such a project requires high ambitions as to its aim and range as well as modesty regarding the prospects of its realisation in the near future. We certainly should not let our expectations run too high. Theories, after all, are no more than didactic models: summaries of the present state of knowledge, aimed primarily at transmitting the general principles as efficiently as possible (cf. Kuhn, 1970). Only by keeping our theoretical perspective flexible and open can this task be performed. We must not strive toward a closed system designed, like Ronald Reagan's chimera of an impenetrable SDI-shield, to intercept any problem. But neither are we empty-handed, even at this date and stage.

Chapter Two

Extensive Growth in the Pre-Modern World

E. L. Jones

This chapter is concerned with the underlying long-term trend of the world economy rather than the usual stuff of economic history, its recent fluctuations. The conventional wisdom is that the entire world economy was stagnant in all material respects until the industrial revolution. Although it is admitted that there were changes these are taken to have been cycles of little lasting economic significance—they are seen as the counterparts of the inconclusive wheeling in Milton's battles of the kites and crows. However, Goudsblom's precept that nothing is ever self-evident (see page 63 below) would lead us to question the interpretation of pre-industrial economic activity as directionless.

Alongside the standard, ultimately stagnationist view it is widely, and somewhat inconsistently, realised that in the long run technical, scientific and even cultural lore did accumulate. This is shrugged off on the grounds that gross distributional inequities denied the average person a benefit. Such a view is beside the immediate point, which is that major implications would follow from demonstrating that total output and income grew, never mind what happened to the average.

What is urged here is that overall output has been rising for several millenia at least.[1] The world was not connected in a single economic system until quite recently but it is still interesting that we can detect a net historical tendency in its economic aggregates. It indicates that output in zones of expansion was steadily outperforming output in zones of stasis and contraction. We are on reasonably safe ground in asserting a growth in the total with respect to the last three thousand years, perhaps longer, although this is a period which has seldom been treated as a whole. Over that span of time the interest of the archæologist or prehistorian more or less fades before that of the historian picks up. During the period the predominant form of economic growth was *extensive* growth, meaning that total rather than per capita output and income went up. Interesting questions follow: what produced the tendency; what impeded a flow-on to *intensive* growth (rising annual real output and income per capita); and what were the implications for the eventual achievement of *intensive* growth, since the background was expansionary, not stagnant after all.

Any account of economic history which is concerned with abstractions of this order over the whole world during several thousand years is bound to be schematic. If the account claims, as this does, that there was continual net change at the global level, it must seem to speed up glacially slow reality and overrun the known instances of economic retreat so as to appear like a jerky silent film. The analogy is close in that individual actors do not get a chance to speak. Nevertheless there are advantages which would be eroded by elaborating the account to discuss the fate of individual states or social movements in the usual fashion of histories. The advantages boil down mainly to those of a bird's-eye view in which broad patterns and long trends are visible whereas in the customary close-up they may be dilated out of sight. Notwithstanding this, there is meant to be room in the scheme to fit in the preponderant facts, the examples of the central tendencies of the economic past.

1. Veils Round the Pre-modern World

A demarcation line or sometimes a hiatus between the interests of prehistorians and economic historians is not the only reason why the last three thousand years or similar tracts are seldom treated as single blocks of time, with effects fatal to the recognition of *extensive* growth. From our position in time the entire history of the pre-modern world is obscured by a number of veils.

For a start, we live after the spread of industrialisation. Even what we think of as remnant agricultural societies, which hint at what the peasant past may have been like, are touched by it. Indeed, they are clenched in the fist of the world industrial market economy. We have a better general model of market economies than non-market ones because we do not have a good general appreciation of the state as an economic system. Indeed, as Perry Anderson (1974b: 404) has pointed out, pre-capitalist economies were less alike than capitalist ones: there has been a capitalist convergence.

We live, too, after the demographic transition which has lifted humanity out of the high birth rate/high death rate pressure cooker—or, as some think, made the cooker blow up.

Further, we post-date the era of Western Imperialism, the '1497-1947' era which refashioned the extra-European world. Europe's empires, held in a cat's cradle of sea-lanes, distract attention from the history of the land empires which formed world affairs far longer.

All these things make our perception of the pre-modern world misty. Our view of it also recedes very rapidly. According to a study by Taagepera and Colby (1979: 907–12) of the history of encyclopaedias, which they take as summing up the perceived relative significance of knowledge, historical writing suffers from a steep and uniform rate of discount. As we go back in time, successively earlier periods receive less space. This is apparently on the assumption that the relevance or present value of the past is perfectly correlated with its nearness to us. It is a somewhat arbitrary assumption. Early periods of great technical change or institution building, perhaps the establishment of whole new cultures, may have been more formative than humdrum later times.

Demographic history definitely shares this recency bias, together with a yen for an exactitude seldom obtainable even in the developed countries before the census in the nineteenth century. According to one of them, Durand (1977: 253), demographers have a myopic view of history stemming from an excessive concern with measurements more precise than our macro-economic models can cope with or strictly need. According to two others, McEvedy and Jones (1978: 358), historical demographers like best writing papers—'long papers, on small subjects, with no conclusions. Hunting about for the few that are relevant to a simple study like ours is an exhausting business.' What is more, the short-period bias in demography seems to have bred an excessive interest in the social controls keeping fertility and mortality in balance, i.e. a positively economics-like concern with equilibria. In the *very* long term the world demographic condition has been one of *disequilibrium*, or the total population would not have kept growing. The equilibria to

which premodern populations supposedly insisted on returning lay on
an ever-rising curve.

The list of motes in our eyes is quite long. Our view of world history,
or as Goudsblom would prefer, human history, suffers from the
parcellement of nationalism. This is largely the result of Western
historiography, self-absorbed, prone to treat that peculiarly Western
creation the nation-state as the natural unit of human affairs.
This political box has been exported so as to form a grid over the
whole surface of the earth. Non-Western parochialisms and insularities
have done nothing to prevent the format being adopted in the writing
of their own histories.

Yet even in Europe the nation-state does not have a particularly long
history. The history of whoever happened to live in an area currently
bounded by the frontiers of a nation-state is not at all the same thing.
Writing that is to commit an anachronism, to fake the ancestry of the
nation and the state as some people have been known to fake their
family trees. The most serious consequence is to shatter the mirror that
was formerly held up to global, or human, history. Seventeenth- and
eighteenth-century scholars were properly interested in the whole world,
or all humanity, as well as its parts. The looking-glass they used needs
to be glued together again if we are to detect the broad trends.
Fortunately, the revival of 'world history' to which this volume is a
contribution suggests that this is happening.

All these impediments to a clear, far-seeing and complete view of the
human past are influenced by the values of the observer. I do not imply
wilful kinds of blinkering, much less that there is one dominating
ideology. Studies of single aspects of the past, from a particular
direction, are appropriate in their place. Nevertheless taken together
they do blur whole world trends like the trend of *extensive* growth.
Even to seek for something like this has been suspected as condoning
growth for its own sake. There is a *non sequitur* here. It is by no means
necessary to approve of something in order to think it important enough
to study: who except neo-Nazis or Marxists could otherwise write the
histories of Auschwitz or the Gulag Archipelago? Like mass in-
carcerations, growth is something the historian can observe. I happen
to view one with horror and the other with qualified approbation but
the questions about both are the standard trinity of (social) scientific
ones: What caused them? What did they involve? What were their

effects? The answers ought to be as dispassionate as we can make them. We can and should allow explicitly for the influence of our own beliefs, as part of the long-standing search for inter-personal knowledge.

It had scarcely occurred to me, before some non-economists in the Exeter seminar said so, that other scholars might not agree that economic growth (meaning primarily the *intensive* growth which characterises most of the world today) is a 'good thing' and will be so for any foreseeable future.[2] After all it is a maxim of welfare economics that more income is better than less. Achieving the 'stationary' economy that is sometimes talked about—stationary, that is, in terms of average income per head—would be possible only if the number of downwardly mobile losers balanced the gainers. There is no chance that all incomes can be held rigidly constant, over the life cycle for instance. Even trying to rig the books so as to maintain a net balance, with its gainer/loser implications, would be abhorrent to me, requiring as it would the imposition of force by the state. We have seen the deleterious effects of income rigidity on incentives in Brezhnev's USSR, and even there strict income equality was not the goal of the *nomenklatura*.

The arguments for growth have been stated by Sir Arthur Lewis (1955) and Professor Beckerman (1974). They seem clear in terms of minimising the number of dead babies and giving everyone the widest possible choice, including the choice of leisure. The negative externalities of growth, which are more widely discussed than its benefits, are actually unintended outputs of given technological forms of production. They can and should be dealt with by changes in price incentives and the institutional structure. They are seldom as widespread as critics contend (this is another result of the common lack of a global perspective), nor (despite inevitable trade-offs) do they *ipso facto* negate the material and social value of growth.

2. The Case for *Extensive* Growth

The logic of the case that *extensive* growth has characterised the world economy for a very long time is that the rise of population must carry up with it total output, which implies total income. For this to be so we need make only a minimal assumption regarding the initial annual average level of per capita real income, i.e. that it was very low, offering little room for any fall to offset a rise in the total produced by population growth. This assumption seems reasonable for the largely agricultural world of three thousand years ago. In my view it would also be reasonable for the world of hunter-gatherers but this is more contentious in view of romantic opinions about their life-style. Observations about that are not part of the case here, neither for the moment is any particular view taken as to whether it was population growth that pushed up total output or whether population was pulled up by output growth. Given that no decline in average real output per head would have been sufficient to cancel out the total effect of prolonged population growth, it follows that *extensive* growth did take place. The increase of population tracks a lower-bound for the growth of total output.

We possess estimates within appropriate bounds of plausibility which show that world population climbed 1700 per cent. from 50 million in 1000 BC to 900 million in AD 1800 (McEvedy and Jones, 1978: 343–4). That is an annual growth rate of 0.103 per cent. The most comprehensive and convenient source, the work of McEvedy and Jones, gives estimates which show that aggregate world population has grown for at least seven or eight thousand years. Since AD 500, at any rate, the aggregate growth has not paused for as much as a century. McEvedy and Jones claim that the indifference range, where there is no reason to prefer one figure over another, was no greater than ± 10 per cent. as far back as AD 1. They further calculate that the rate of growth reached its prehistoric peak about 1000 BC, at the start of the Iron Age in Europe and the Near East, approximately the date when we will start our own survey. Although the rate slackened for a time thereafter it remained positive and absolute numbers continued to climb as they had been doing and have done ever since.

It seems to be because rates of growth were low by the standards of very recent and atypical centuries and because there were marked variations in individual regions of the globe that the significance of the prolonged positive trend has been skated over. The doubling time has certainly been dropping. The total took from the start of the Christian era to the early fifteenth century to achieve one doubling; the next took only until 1750; the next again until 1890. This concentrates interest on the acceleration in the industrial era but it should be of deep interest that there was trend acceleration long before that.

Population growth without any sign of a long-term fall in life expectancy satisfies Guha's (1981) criteria for economic growth. These take human numbers and length of life as less chimerical indicators than utility maximisation, where the goal indicator for currently-preferred goods shifts up in Stakhanovite fashion with every advance. The criteria are (a) rising life expectancy with population constant, or (b) rising population with life expectancy constant, or (c) both climbing together. There are no satisfactory early data on life expectancy but for what they are worth the fragmentary samples collected by Dublin, Lotka and Spiegelman (1936) from Bronze Age and Iron Age Greece, Rome, medieval England and New England about AD 1800 imply an increase in life expectancy at birth from interval to interval over the whole period.

Coupled with the *extensive* growth inherent in overall population growth starting from a low income base this implies that the world economy has been expanding for a very long time. There were more people for a start, while even if average real income per capita did not rise on an annual basis, the average person may have come to live longer. This does not mean that there was *intensive* growth in quite the modern sense but it does suggest something subtly more than the minimum *extensive* growth criterion of greater total income. Perhaps we could call the *very* long-term average condition one of '*extensive* growth plus'. This is consistent with the evidence of capital formation and economic activity in general. An eventual sea-change is indicated, overlooked though it has been.

Larger numbers and densities of people, with a slow swelling of output, necessarily expanded other variables. The context of all subsequent growth was increasing net investment and continual experience with technical change. The area cultivated had to rise at least in proportion to population, unless agricultural methods improved, which would be of interest in itself. The reality was a little of each: the areas occupied and cultivated rose and in major regions of the world agricultural tools, crop strains and species, and farming methods did all improve.

Agricultural intensification occurred in response to population growth even without the improvements in technique which we will in any case shortly describe. As Ester Boserup (1965) proposed, in agricultural systems with relatively little market activity the cycle of shifting agriculture became shorter and ultimately it was fixed to the spot. Whatever the trend of marginal returns to effort, that is output per person as opposed to output per hectare, there was the floor of subsistence needs underneath. This means that total output could go on swelling commensurately with the swelling of human numbers.

Capital in premodern times resided largely in cleared and fenced fields; herds and flocks of farm animals; and buildings of all kinds. We have nothing that passes for global estimates of these. Nevertheless it is not only the logic of the thing which guarantees that they did increase. We have an extensive literature on the spread and greater densities of human populations; on conquests, frontier movements, and settlement histories; on vast irrigation works; and a considerable archæology of buildings.

Despite this, the overall rate of capital formation was undoubtedly low. It is an easy sentence to write and easy to believe. But without the qualification, 'by modern standards', it means little. Base-weighted in the long ago in order to observe what happened over time, rather than foreshortened by putting the base in the historically-abnormal present, the salient fact is that the rate was positive rather than that it was low. For all the episodes of destruction, retreat and genocide, there is no real doubt that the three thousand years before AD 1800 saw an enormous net accumulation of capital embodied in land improvements, in buildings and in some other guises such as tools. Even very low rates, where they were invested in productive assets rather than in ceremonial structures, accumulated nicely over the length of time we have at our disposal.

Few people have ventured to cite numbers, though Goldsmith is a recent and valuable exception.[3] If we turn to the output side, to overall rates of growth in product per head, even Patel's (1964) figure of 'less than' 0.1 per cent per annum would mean that an annual share of total product of $50 per capita in 1000 BC would have become $821 p.a. by AD 1800. The rate of 0.1 per cent p.a. derives from Keynes's essay on 'Economic Possibilities for our Grandchildren' (1951) and seems to be nothing more than an illustration or guess.

Goldsmith's figure of 0.2 per cent p.a. (1987: 233), which has the backing of the author's careful regional studies, would convert the same initial sum into $13,446 by AD 1800. That did not come about, of course. Goldsmith's phrasing at this point is untypically obscure. He may mean that the rate of growth of national product was no more than 0.2 per cent p.a. for periods of decades even when particular societies were doing well. It may have been lower, indeed it must have been lower, the remainder of the time, at least over the average of all societies. For instance, he thinks that the per capita share of national product in Mughal India in 1700 was about $200 (in $US of 1970), about three-quarters of the then British, French and colonial American level. But the population of Mughal India was five times greater than the combined total of these other countries (Goldsmith, 1987: 102; McEvedy and Jones, 1978, passim.).

Keynes, who was so impressed by the power of compound interest, does not seem to have made much of the fact that the length of period he was discussing would offset, *ceteris paribus*, the lowness of its annual rate of growth. Nor did he make much of the need for a powerful explanation of why *any* positive rate did not result in a large final total. The time-span is so great that minute variations in percentage growth rates, could they be sustained, would have made an enormous difference to the final figure. The rub is that they could not be sustained on the world scale, despite the evidence of innovative and expansionary activity.

Technical change in agriculture is undoubted. The stock of knowledge about productive techniques has been embodied in formal as well as informal sources for a long time back. The very term 'Iron Age' marks a major diffusion of relevant lore. In Europe and China it came to be written in textbooks and *Nongshu* and updated from age to age. There were immense transfers of crop species and productive varieties. Consider three examples: the Arab Agricultural Revolution which from the seventh century AD carried sixteen food crops from India as far west as Spain; the spread of Champa rice from Indo-China from the eleventh century and the successive rediffusions in China and Japan of strains that ripened earlier and earlier; and the 'Columbian Exchange' through which not only were European crops and livestock established in the Americas but in return maize, peanuts, sweet potatoes and white potatoes rapidly penetrated the agricultures of Europe, Africa and China. The productivity effects of these technology transfers are well known. A wider range of cultivated species reduced the risks of harvest failure and acted as a demographic buffer. White potatoes for example were valuable in the hitherto climatically marginal northern tier of Europe while maize was useful in the dry Mediterranean basin.

Over the period there was similarly a disproportionate growth of cities. 'Premodern history,' declares Rozman (1973: 13), 'can be seen as successive additions of new levels of cities.' During the three thousand years to AD 1800 the share of the world's population living in cities of over 10,000 inhabitants went up from less than one per cent to four or even six or seven per cent.[4] Ten thousand is of course a high threshold for premodern urbanism and probably does not faithfully indicate the scale of the withdrawal of labour from primary production. The increase has been dwarfed by the subsequent helter-skelter urbanisation but viewed fairly it represented a considerable change in its own right. This may have taken a long time yet the urban proportion was much greater at the end than at the beginning: he who laughs last laughs longest.

Urbanisation can be seen as part of a process of structural change, in which more and more labour shifted from less productive primary occupations like farming to more productive secondary (manufacturing) and tertiary (service) activities. This is consistent with an *absolute* rise in agricultural employment while nevertheless a smaller *fraction* of the population remained on the land to feed an increasing number and proportion of city dwellers. Better communications and marketing arrangements were also involved. While this structural shift has been eclipsed by nineteenth- and twentieth-century industrialisation, once again it represented a profound economic change on its own terms.

There was yet another profound *very* long-term change, this time in the size of political units. Work by McEvedy and Jones (1978) and Taagepera (1978) shows that the largest empire in the world was always greater in both area and population than the previous holder of the title.[5] This conclusion is based on careful measurements of the geographical extent and estimates of population in successive empires. The empire was the typical large political unit of this phase of human history. In spite of the attention which, ever since Ibn Khaldun's day, the fall of empires has drawn to the dynastic cycle, the underlying trend of growth in unit size is conspicuous. In the literature there occurs the notion of an equilibrium size of political unit, a point at which costs and benefits balance, but like those of premodern populations these equilibria lay on a rising scale.[6] The long-run condition of world society has been disequilibrium.

Despite a degree of obscurity surrounding the relationship between size of polity and *extensive* economic growth, a few suggestions may be made about possible connections. First, despite the slaughter associated with initial conquests, the internal order imposed by a single ruler quickly fostered population growth and economic activity. Secondly, some empires made strenuous efforts to promote economic stability by counter-disaster measures such as ever-normal granaries. The role of the premodern ruler typically included an insurance function of this kind; by the eighteenth century AD the measures in China in particular were most effective, having been developing on lines laid down under the Sung eight or nine centuries earlier.[7] Thirdly, international trade flourished best when it could take place between extensive, stable units, as in Han-Parthian-Roman or T'ang-Abassid times (Curtin, 1984).

Most interesting of all, the 'mean time to failure' of empires seems to have fallen in prehistoric times but become longer again during the Christian era. Between 2,800 BC–610 BC, the first nine of a sample of eighteen empires shrank below 80 per cent of their maximum extent after an average of 260 years whereas for the last nine this took only 110 years.[8] Much later, the Asian empires supposedly damaged by Western imperialism were not only bigger than their predecessors but lasted longer. A way to rescue an hypothesis of Western malignity might be by arguing that those which survived did so because the Western powers propped them up. For the Ottoman empire, the 'sick man of Europe' during the nineteenth century, this rings true enough, though by then the Ottomans were shedding territories and population. The same is not plausible with respect to Manchu China, the largest land empire of them all. Over the long haul of human history, empires—or top empires—had tended to expand in size and population.

In sum, what we observe in respect of *extensive* growth is first its *sine qua non*, the *very* long-term increase in population; secondly, ample evidence of agricultural expansion and intensification, together with the growth of cities, meaning all told a rise in world capital stock; and thirdly an expansion in the area, population and longevity of the largest political unit. The relationship between politics and economics cut both ways. Political expansion seems to have favoured economic expansion even though it was also associated with the more familiar stagnation of per capita real income. These trends and relationships are detectable very far back in time, with noteworthy signs of accelerating gigantism in polities and economies during the eight hundred years or thereabouts before the classic industrial revolution of the eighteenth century AD.

None of the fluctuations, regressions, or cycles of history was sufficient to halt or reverse the average trend of *extensive* growth. In a series of larger and larger regions of the earth investment growth prevailed—on average. Likewise, states arose—and rose. Tainter (1988: 3) notes that the rise of the state has received far more attention than the fall. That is understandable. In the long haul political expansion and recrudescence have dominated collapse. One hesitates to categorise major events such as the Fall of Rome as little local difficulties but to do so might dramatise the point.[9] Furthermore, as Tainter observes, Dark Ages were seldom sombre for everyone. Distant trade may have suffered from the collapse of imperial order; total farm output and on-the-spot consumption did not necessarily follow suit. What is odd is that this has not been thought of as an aspect of the underlying economic phenomenon: the ratchet effect of economic expansion has not received attention comparable to that lavished on the fortunes of the state.

3. Causes

The issue is, what was responsible for the *extensive* growth tendency? Given the central role we have assigned to population it may be thought that an intrinsic biological urge in our species was responsible. The natural history or social biology of our species has certainly gained a vogue (Mackenzie, 1978). One can identify any number of motives, along the lines of old age insurance, why the majority class of peasants may have chosen to form families and produce sizeable broods of children. I have counted seven distinct reasons in the literature and some of these may have operated in combination. But such reasons tend to be social or economic as much or more than biological; it is by no means clear that humanity inherently prefers to maximise numbers rather than income per head, or by virtue of biology alone is in a position to maximise either. It is not self-evident that we are or have been in the grip of some biological or demographic 'manifest destiny' that must lead to numbers above replacement. Whatever the urge, social conditions affect whether it will be manifest.

It takes two to tango: both humanity and environment, the latter including competing peoples. Despite the adaptability of *Homo sapiens* there seems no certainty that the environment or inter-specific competition (i.e. other people) must sanction unending population growth. Admittedly determinism of the control-by-sunspots kind is not quite dead. Climatic historians are most tempted by it, though nowadays they tend to dance away from the implications of their earlier statements.[10] Even Braudel's allusion to population fluctuations in China, India and Europe being synchronised by unobserved fluctuations in the jet stream, 'as if all humanity was in the grip of a primordial cosmic destiny in relation to which the rest of its history would be truly secondary,' (quoted by Cameron, 1970: 457) is protected by its rhetorical 'as if' phrase.

There does seem to be one biological mechanism which permits human populations to jump upwards at intervals. This is the crossing of thresholds when a population has 'tamed' some disease organism, relegating it from a serious hazard to a nursery ill. A succession of these relegations can be documented (McNeill, 1976). The exposure of populations to new diseases introduces some of the characteristic discontinuities of 'real world' history, as when the Black Death spread with the trade under the Pax Mongolica: the demographic consequences were out of all proportion to the tiny commerce between Asia and Europe. Pandemics may thus account for some of the hesitations in premodern demographic growth. The process was non-linear as well as not really predictable. The world has reached the stage of microbial unification only relatively recently (Ladurie, 1973). Nevertheless here is an apparently biological process which seemingly gives rise to the conditions for a series of demographic spurts. A snag for biological fundamentalism is however that it required changing *social* conditions, in this case trade links, to spread the disease organisms.

One way of approaching the issue of causation is to note that neither the trend of *extensive* growth as depicted by the course of population nor the trend in the size of the largest political unit was uniform through time. Both were subject to irregularities, including an occasional brief downturn but more conspicuously some plateaus. Patently the forces driving these trends ran out of steam after periods of some centuries but subsequently recouped—or others took over—and pushed upwards again. Although this might be consistent, admittedly, with variation in biological or climatic influences, it opens the way for an alternative interpretation. Cycles are also consistent with the history of social innovation, and that is better documented than the cloudy assertions of climatic or *Ur*-biological causality.

Taagepera for example has suggested historical developments that may account for the observed renewals of the expansion path of empire. He associated a sudden increase in the area of the largest empire about 2,800 BC with the emergence of cities; about 600 BC with the discovery of the means of delegating power; and about AD 1600 with a revolution in the speed of communication. At times the conquerors sopped up more advanced technical and administrative methods from those they had overrun and then generalised them over wider areas: examples cited by Clough are Greece and Rome, the Manchu in China and the Aztecs who took from the Toltecs what they had taken in turn from the Maya (Clough, 1961). Discontinuities like these hint that changes in social and economic organisation are not simply reflexive responses to growing numbers but have to be socially constructed, may be diffused, and are subject to diminishing returns. In principle, once *extensive* growth is disaggregated it is likely to prove amenable to economic analysis.

What seems most likely is that the major variations in population, size of political unit, and total output were at base the result of different combinations of innovations in methods of production, distribution, communications and political management. In other words, what is being observed are economic and political innovations, none of infinitely lasting potency, all finally subject to diminishing marginal returns. When the gains to any given cluster of techniques began to fall off, there was a pause until some other novelty took up the slack.

The essence is that, taking the world economy as a whole, combined technical and structural changes kept output up with the growth of population. Measured over more than individual macro-regions and short cycles of time, the world was not Malthusian. Great regional famines there were, but it has now been shown that their demographic impact was far less than historians have always thought; the imprint of the greatest recorded famine lasted only a tiny fraction of the length of our period and then only in a given region (Menken and Watkins, 1985).

At the global level, improvements in agricultural method kept just a mite ahead of the growth of human numbers. Let us continue to call this *extensive* growth plus. The increasing returns needed to achieve *intensive* growth were harder to attain or sustain. They were not however quite so hard that the world could be transformed only once, by the European industrial revolution.[11] Taking into account the giant disequilibria caused by our species entering and re-entering more and more unoccupied niches, the *very* long-term average may have been constant returns.

Already at the start of our period few areas of the world entirely lacked people. The expansionary process involved better-equipped, better-organised societies recolonising less densely settled areas, while less disturbed populations gradually intensified their methods of production. This, then, was an economic and political rather than biological process, brought about by groups whose power and numbers had been augmented by successful technical or organisational change.

Certainly the process can be seen in its biological aspect as a modification of habitats. By and large each change made subsequent ones easier: even the aboriginal inhabitants of the neo-Europes studied by Crosby brought about so many changes in flora and fauna that the subsequent entry of European agricultural colonists was greatly facilitated (Crosby, 1986). Earlier historiography missed the significance of this pre-European landscape modification, which we can now see as a slow enhancement of what the classical economists called 'capital-in-land.' For all the episodic upsets of history, the positive changes—the movements of peoples, greater average density of settlement, upgrading of methods, and conversion of more and more land to arable—resulted in an accumulation of capital, in short in material progress.

Progress is a distinctly unfashionable term nowadays when general historians make everything of the initial costs to aborigines of white settlement and nothing of the later gains. However the European expansion represented only another phase in the long saga of the intensification of economic activity, a *recolonisation*. Because of its closeness to us in time and political importance, it tends to obscure prior movements, yet it was not new in principle. Stand back far enough, as we can from the end of three thousand years, and progress—material progress—is a reasonable description of the trend.

Structural change was more than a proportionate response to population growth. The rise of cities and increase in non-agricultural employment meant that labour was being released from farming. How was this done? Improvements in agricultural method must have been moderately labour-saving. Indeed in most sectors there were continual diffusions of technique, moving like glaciers but moving just the same. The westward spread of Chinese knowledge has been studied in greatest detail. As Glick (1979: 22, 132) has remarked, the Islamic Middle East, broker between Asia and Europe, rejected Chinese science but welcomed Chinese technologies which could more easily be dissociated from any suspect ideological baggage. For many societies some fraction of technical change was thus exogenous. Boserup (1981) has also suggested that productivity gains were made endogenously because the big labour forces recruited to build irrigation works achieved economies of scale.

More fundamentally, technological change in general may have been weakly endogenous, an unintended by-product of everyday practice. Persson (1988) has formally urged as much for Europe. He believes that slowly accumulating technical knowledge was handed down from generation to generation in settled rural communities. The rate of change was governed by the extent of the division of labour, hence by the size of the market, and this in turn by the size of population. In this fashion the long-run growth of human numbers would automatically bring about technical change, sluggish but slowly speeding up, because it widened the market, increased the division of labour and multiplied the chances of assimilating new skills by force of repetition.

There are difficulties with the Persson thesis. At the conceptual level it is not clear why social institutions, including property rights, should not have played a major part in affecting the rate of technical change. On the empirical front the larger populations do not necessarily seem to have been those with the fastest rates of change and in addition there were undoubted regressions in technique at times. Nevertheless in a general sense the thesis sits well with the history of invention and innovation.

Elements of different explanations of *extensive* growth are lurking here. One is a demand-side explanation which simply assumes a tendency for population to grow and feed itself. In Boserupian fashion agricultural intensification responds to the rise of population, and population grows subject only to intermittent shocks as isolated populations come into contact and suffer mortality from unfamiliar diseases. The shock-wave of mortality caused by the initial European expansion to the neo-Europes of the Americas, the Pacific Islands and Australasia is the best-known example.[12] In general however the process is self-fulfilling, almost automatic, driven by population growth.

This does not however readily account for structural change. The alternative explanation is a supply-side one: that the global cycles of population and total output mark the diffusion of successive levels of technique, each eventually succumbing to the onset of diminishing returns. Even McEvedy and Jones, who turn to climatic change to account for the downturn in their primary population cycle about AD 200, invoke European technology and imperialism to explain the cycle from the fifteenth century AD.

A neat fit between particular complexes of farming method and world population cycles is admittedly hard to establish. For example, the food producing effects of the Discoveries, that is of the Columbian Exchange and the new lands available to cultivate, were so lagged that they cannot have been the cause of the gain in total human numbers during the fifteenth and sixteenth centuries. Their main effects awaited the development of oceanic transport in the nineteenth century. One possibility is that the population growth of the early modern period was merely a bounce-back from the Black Death, supported by creeping, overlapping diffusions of better farming methods. Agricultural history has scarcely been written at the appropriate level, let alone assembled on a world scale, and there are many patterns we cannot yet detect. Of the population growth and *extensive* growth there is no real doubt.

The cycles were like the risers and treads of a staircase. Perhaps demand- and supply-side motors took over from one another to produce this result. Wave-like diffusions of new technology may have pushed up output (and pulled up population) until diminishing returns set in. Thereafter population growth fed itself at more-or-less static levels, and continued to replicate existing technology, until another 'wave of gadgets' swelled. The term wave of gadgets is by courtesy of T.S. Ashton's schoolboy; wave is a little dramatic and gadgets should be taken to include new institutional arrangements.

4. Impediments to *Intensive* Growth

Given a degree of technical advance and structural change, what impeded transitions to *intensive* growth? Not excessive population growth, since this was vastly slower than modern rates and would not have imposed unbearable dependency ratios. The basic impediments seem rather to have lain in the intensely hierarchical politics characteristic of premodern times. Goldsmith has made some calculations of the inequalities of wealth and income in seven premodern societies, of which three are probably representative of the larger empires before each began to decay (Goldsmith, 1987: Table 12–1). His figures show that the top one-thousandth of all families in Augustan Rome in AD 14 received four per cent. of total income. In the Ottoman empire about AD 1550 the share was fifteen per cent. The top ten-thousandth of families received one per cent. of income in the Roman case and five per cent. in Mughal India about AD 1600. For comparison, the top ten-thousandth of families in both India and England in the late 1970s received only—if that is the word—0.1 per cent. of income. In the United States their share was 0.25 per cent. Those figures are still ten and twenty-five times the equilibrium shares but they contrast very favourably with one hundred times in Rome and five hundred times in Mughal India.

Not much of the disproportionate share of wealth and income in so few hands in the premodern world was reinvested productively. Instead it was spent on luxury, display and the militarism needed to extract a surplus from one's own people, as well as to extract rents by conquering others. Although rational for ruling groups and conquerors, this was a slicing of existing pies: it did little to help bake them. That the rate of capital accumulation was so low by modern standards is partly explained by this: the heaping up of capital in the *very* long term which happened is explained by the length of time involved. Most people had very little left over from their ordinary needs to invest and little incentive to take risks; in these circumstances the noteworthy fact is that net investment did keep expanding, however slowly.

The great inequalities hint at their own explanation and at the explanation of how few were the instances of *intensive* growth. They point to the fierce social and political controls that locked premodern economies into rounds of mere *extensive* growth. Yet, as we have urged throughout, in itself that was an achievement. The premodern world was not one of utter economic stagnation but a prolonged unfolding which added up to *extensive* growth plus, though it seldom tipped over in any region into a growth of average per capita incomes. Seldom: but not just in the one industrial revolution. The economic context was slightly more propitious than that. Admittedly, the world economy as a whole seems not to have grown in the per capita income sense. On the other hand, population growth and technical change did impart a momentum of continual expansion.

Chapter Three

Recurrent Transitions to *Intensive* Growth

The central task of economic history is to explain transitions from
extensive growth to *intensive* growth. All else is commentary. The small
number of spontaneous examples of *intensive* growth implies that
transition was a surpassingly difficult matter. Yet all parts of the bridge
were not equally hard to build. Although history is niggardly with clues
as to which were the hardest parts, the prelude of *extensive* growth
suggests that achieving a sustained rise in average per capita GNP ought
not to have been preternaturally formidable. In the premodern world
there was technical change and what might be called 'investment creep.'
The need was not to crank up completely cold economies but to pass
already warm ones, in which total output and income were expanding,
through the phase transition to the point where average income per
head was growing. The normal explanations, embodied in industrial
revolution studies, are inclined to talk as though the achievement burst
on an economically-stagnant world. They tend to be couched in terms
of novel push-forces. Here the aim will be to look for a different type
of explanation.

1. The East Asian Growth Pole

First, however, we need to discard the assumption that the transition
was so very difficult that it happened spontaneously on a unique
occasion: in eighteenth-century Britain. To think so succeeds in confusing (among other things) growth with industrialisation. There was
in any case more than one focus of growth in the world, as there is

today. Alongside the Western world of Europe and its overseas annexes there is now an East Asian complex which is growing faster; possesses the larger financial market; and perhaps least acknowledged has a longer if somewhat more interrupted history. Treating East Asia as entirely derivative, as is usual, traps us inside the diffusionist interpretation that traces all growth back to the industrial revolution and impedes our understanding of the process of growth in the round.

The common approach to East Asian growth in general economic histories is to restrict it to Japan on the grounds that growth anywhere else in the region is extraordinarily recent. Furthermore, the Japanese experience tends to be assimilated to that of the West—to the point of labelling Japan 'Western'—along one or other of the following lines: (1) the diligence and thrift enjoined by Japanese ideals are taken to be an ersatz version of the Protestant Ethic. Enough said: that brings growth. (2) Japan, like Europe, happened to be feudal. Again, enough said: feudalism eventually self-transforms into bourgeois capitalism, assumed in turn to produce growth. (3) The Meiji Restoration of 1868 brought about a growth some suppose to have been lacking in Japan hitherto. The new regime adopted industrialism in order to join a West it could not otherwise keep at bay. (4) Japan really achieved growth only after her prostration in 1945—by emulating, and later outclassing, the industrial practices of her American occupiers.

These interpretations, some more than others, allude to real historical events and processes. The construction placed on each of them depends however on making Japanese economic history a variant or descendant of Western economic history, which is regarded as the *fons et origo* of all true growth. If one is thinking only with respect to industrialisation, or with modern magnitudes and modern rates of change in mind, it is easy to slip into the same habit. The choices of 1868 or 1945 as turning-points are attempts to define the Japanese adoption of Western industrialism. Either date begins a diffusionist tale. The explanations in terms of feudalism or religious behaviour are more ingenious without however elaborating much on the economic effects. They offer Japan (and Japan alone among non-Western nations) access to growth on lines sanctioned by the study of Western history.

That Japanese talents were purely imitative was a prevalent opinion in the West in the 1930s, with allegations that Japan's industrial wares were routinely stamped 'Made in Birmingham' or some such. Perhaps they were: access to the protected markets of Western colonial empires in Asia was limited. We shall argue instead that Japan's growth was distinct from Europe's and arose primarily because the political structure imposed by the Tokugawa evolved to permit it. It was really in the middle reaches, from the Meiji Restoration to the early Showa era, that Japan borrowed factory industrialism from the West. The earlier evolution was like that of the West, but quite independent; what Meiji did was to give a massive statist and westernising boost to already active market forces. What late Showa did, after the Second World War, was to beat the masters at their own game.

The outcome is Japan's world prominence, so colossal that some might be led to switch allegiance and turn Japanese studies into a monotheism to replace that of the industrial revolution. Within the East Asian sphere, Japan's scale could easily distort the study of economic history, unless we think determinedly about causes and rates of change rather than magnitudes. Consider: Japan's share of world GNP is approaching America's; her share of world exports is almost there. Vast Japanese capital transfers are vital to the United States. Japan has the largest bank in the world, the largest financial institution, and the largest company. Japan's tiny land area is valued at approximately twice the value of the United States. And so on.[1]

Despite this, if we want to understand how growth starts rather than how it may attain hypertrophy, the appropriate sphere of enquiry is East Asia as a whole. In particular, notice should be taken of the dynamic phases of Chinese history. At first sight this seems a blind alley since again 'everyone knows' that until the last couple of decades economic success in Asia was granted only to Japan. There are however at least three ways of revolving the lens to display a different picture. One, to which we shall briefly refer again, is to consider that the economic condition of Manchu China was not quite as unpromising as most accounts surmise. That means ceasing to dismiss early periods as irrelevant before we have looked to see whether or not they really are. Another is to adjust the reportedly low growth rates to take account of gains in life expectancy (Usher, 1973). There is every reason to think that the result would be to show much greater percentage gains since at the least 1949 than are revealed by conventional income measures alone. The third approach we have already mooted: decoupling growth from industrialisation in order to search for the inception of growth as such. Comparing the histories of *intensive* growth in Europe and East Asia depends in the first instance on which European chronology is adopted. Contradictory opinions are expressed, or more often implicit assumptions are made, as to whether growth came early or came late, came fast or came slow. The opinion of the quantifiers has stretched the industrial revolution towards the present like a cartoon cat, implying that the growth rate of industrial production did not accelerate much until well into the nineteenth century. That school of thought tends to ignore early change, when there are few predigested statistical series. A less articulate view, still apparently held among economic historians, accepts that real wages per head had been growing for centuries, though very slowly and perhaps not continuously, nor outside Britain and the Low Countries. We will incline towards this gradualist view of the timing and to an even broader view of the parts of Europe that were involved.

If the East Asian record is set against this latitudinarian version of the European experience it displays the following characteristics: an earlier start, at least as early as the Sung dynasties (AD 960–1279); an admittedly less continuous record in the sense that the flame flickered and the torch came to be borne by Japan rather than China; a strong rediffusion within East Asia; and nowadays a distinctly faster rate of growth in areas bigger than the biggest European countries. In the literature on world development these characteristics are seldom connected in a coherent sequence. Yet *intensive* growth was Chinese before it was European, and today, although of course the income base is vastly lower, growth rates in some huge provinces of China are again faster than anywhere in Europe. The sceptical Western view is that this cannot last and will not spread; also that the earlier history cannot matter. It has been the bane of development economics to take the short view.

The present chapter urges caution about dismissing China's prospects and disputes the idea that history cannot tell us anything of interest. Consider the extent of economic activity and the remarkable stock of so-called preindustrial techniques in late Manchu China. The political system was decayed and average incomes were undoubtedly low but this does not necessarily denote a society which was backward in all other respects. Viewed more kindly than usual, it was one with a great deal of energy and creativity. It is possible to conceive that what was chiefly required was the breaking of a political log-jam, not the construction of an economic system entirely from scratch. Compared with some parts of the less-developed world, China remained heir to a heritage that had once been most influential and might perhaps be re-activated.

The world historian W. H. McNeill (1982: 24–5), has seen the early picture more clearly than almost anyone. He envisages the original European growth as an epiphenomenon of Sung commercialism. This is the reverse of the West-East direction of economic diffusion in recent centuries. It points to a more appropriate history that embraces sequential hearths of change. This is welcome, since economic history should not take as its goal explaining how any given economy attained a particular equilibrium. The mutability of the past means that it would be inadequate simply to replace a saga which culminates in the British industrial revolution with another which culminates, say, in the present strength of Japan. To do so courts being left high and dry by the next tide of economic leadership.[2] The proper goal is the study of the *process* of change, not constructing a teleology that leads to the transient prominence of this economy or that.

After the Sung, China as a whole reverted for centuries to merely expansionary growth. At least sinologists do not claim otherwise. The regions may have differed but virtually until Republican times there was no clearly-documented return to *intensive* growth overall. However in Japan *intensive* growth picked up. While it has to be taken into account that Japanese culture derived from China, the evolution of her economy was different. Japan's growth may be traced to a slow start during or even before the Tokugawa period. This had massive eventual implications, not only for Japan today but also for growth in the 'Little Dragons' of South Korea and Taiwan. Their development is to an important extent a spin-off from the immensely rapid achievement of modern Japan whose colonies we have noted they once were. The important point is that they are heirs to almost as long a tradition as if they had been Western colonies.

By endeavouring to make room for a separate East Asian focus of growth we duplicate the active economic history we need to know and teach. This makes for greater realism; what it does not do is solve the problem of origins, or more precisely of causes, since—as Marc Bloch objected—origins may muddle beginnings and causes. Two patches of growth instead of a single one have to appear on our map of the world. Does this mean that we should then think that these, and only these, cultures were preadapted for growth? To do so would be even more cumbersome and difficult to believe than continuing to write and teach as though only Europe were preordained to grow.

Any such notion that certain parts of the world were inherently favoured would dissuade us from looking for evidence of other early stirrings of *intensive* growth. There were some instances, however faint. Exclusive concentration on the British or European case has always distracted attention from the possibility of comparable achievements elsewhere and restricted our chances of understanding the fundamental conditions under which *intensive* growth may appear. Including East Asia as well as Europe widens our scope but there is no advantage in entering two blind alleys instead of one.

Europeans and East Asians cannot be shown to have been the world's only creative peoples. That would permit modern results to obliterate past efforts. The very idea is redundant and may be offensive. It is distinctly likely for instance that *intensive* growth emerged in the coastal trading cities or states of southeast Asia during (what was in European terms) the Middle Ages (Reid, 1988). That this episode went into reverse in early modern times is beside the point. For a spell another growth pole was sketched on the map. Comparative work taking into account this and any other tentative examples will be more revealing of the circumstances under which growth arises and can be suppressed than work limited to the history of the great survivors.

This said, three major cases do stand out. They are Sung China (from the 10th–13th century AD), Tokugawa Japan (from 1600–1868), and early modern Europe (from, say, 1500–1800). In each instance the stirrings of still earlier periods ought to be included in a complete account of the inception of growth. We shall be conservative and ignore them here.

We have used the term 'inception.' It would be unfortunate if this reinforced the common assumption of abruptness, of growth 'taking-off'. Another undesirable assumption would be that growth was rare. The relevant processes of technical and institutional change are regarded as having been super-difficult. This impression can be created by the apparent fixity of institutions when incentives were limited, as they were for long stretches of the past: take for example the survival of the guilds in China and the Middle East. Yet in Europe once growth began the guilds lost their teeth quickly enough and there is no reason to suppose that they constituted a more formidable barrier elsewhere (E.L. Jones, 1981, 1988).

Looking over too short a period can also create the impression that growth is immensely difficult. This was the sense conveyed by the literature of development economics for a generation after the Second World War: the apparent sluggishness of development, as seen in close-up, was a convenient stick with which to beat the former colonial powers. Growth may have been frustratingly slow by ideal standards but we can now see that it was historically rapid. It was achieved simultaneously almost everywhere in the world, quite without precedent.

2. Explanations of Growth

Models of growth usually assume the success of one or other novel push force. The postwar experience of the Third World is however a graveyard of hopes that some particular propellant might be effective. Earlier British economic historiography is similarly a cemetery for an array of suggested push forces or positive shocks, none of them fully capable of accounting for growth in its industrial guise let alone as a general process.

The array of proposals in the literature on Britain was not accompanied by any test to determine how we might select among them. Some decades elapsed before it was realised that many of the changes approximately contemporaneous with the industrial revolution were no more than fellow passengers, correlates not causes. Thus the acts of founding of banks or systems of accounting, sometimes portrayed as crucial for growth, were in reality adaptations to it. Banks arose to service an already-swelling volume of transactions. As the realisation dawned that substituting one push force for another in an historical merry-go-round lacked persuasiveness, so the subject lost its fascination as a research field. British economic history marked time with evasive statements about the multiplicity of the forces that led to industrialisation.

Even the underlying hypothesis that growth originated in an industrial revolution—it is no more than an hypothesis—is unhelpful. What it conjures up is a miracle of the laser-beam sort, typically the result of technical change, the steam engine, the spinning jenny, or something of that kind. When change is admitted to have been more gradual it is made dependent on some autonomous cultural change, of which the Protestant Ethic is the major example. But a gradualist stance was never attractive to the economics profession, involved as it was with in-cautious policy advice, as well as with an instrumentalist attitude to knowledge about the past. Certainly economists embraced the notion of a take-off far more closely than did historians. A self-referring element entered the study of development. Bouncing across time like a ping-pong ball, the concept of an abrupt transformation in the past shaped expectations about unheralded development in the present, while the aspirations returned to elicit from history an ever more abrupt curtain-raiser.

No explanation by analogy with the industrial revolution, no merely Western explanation at all, can be general enough to account for the process of economic growth as a whole. It cannot comprehend China and Japan as well as Europe; its ground-rules can only relegate them to the role of offshoots of European growth. In no way can it cope with the realisation that what is to be explained is a number of separate cases, maybe responding to comparable stimuli but not necessarily to common stimuli.

A mental experiment is required. Rather than continue to ransack ever-dustier corners of eighteenth-century Britain for a fresh propellant, let us consider a simpler postulate. Let us assume that a propensity for growth has been widely present in human society. This does not commit us to a 'neoclassical' maximising position. Not everyone need be engaged in maximising on every margin at once. All that is needed is to accept that a desire to reduce material poverty is commonplace in our species, as well it might be considering that poverty exacts such a penalty in terms of dead babies, or at any rate of children without shoes. A certain inquisitiveness about how things work—things, that is, including markets—and a modicum of human creativity are ancillary postulates.

An objection against postulating universal, or rather semi-universal, behaviours like this has been raised by Anne Mayhew (1987). She terms them Elemental Human Strategies. She argues that they must empty the interest from the workings of the economy and distract attention from the institutions which are the proper object of study, the true stuff of history. Despite her institutionalist critique, for which economic historians ought to have some sympathy, other approaches have not produced a persuasive argument. In the circumstances, the assumption of a 'growth propensity' seems worth a trial. Let us see how far it will take us.

Consider the prevalence of attempts to bring about technical change. There is some reason to think that they were the results of a deep inquisitiveness and dexterity that could be and often were stifled or deflected but which in themselves did not have to be created or induced. Technical advances have been described as the result of 'more love than purpose' (Smith, 1981: 330). That love, meaning aesthetics, was more widespread than rationality is surely not hard to believe. In any case Persson has noted a continual slow change in technique in the settled rural societies of European history and he offers a model of technical change as endogenous—weakly endogenous or the outcome would be more noticeable than it is, but endogenous nevertheless (Persson, 1988).

The way that all this was worked out in historical cases was indistinct, and indirect evidence has to be used to assess it. We have neither macro-statistics, apart from those put together by Goldsmith (1987), nor the means—any more than do other economists—of observing motivations directly. The best we can do is to examine material on technological and structural change with our behavioural postulate in mind. Technical change in itself does not guarantee the presence of *intensive* growth but although caveats will have to be entered, it does presuppose vitality. Structural change involves the withdrawal of labour from primary production into the more productive manufacturing and service occupations. If technical and structural change both persisted vigorously for a century or more there is reason to suspect that *intensive* growth was taking place.

Admittedly, much early technical activity was not materially productive. There was more invention than innovation, and invention without insertion into the productive system is sterile. The slogan of Radio Rentals in Australia today illustrates the distinction: 'soon as they invent it, we rent it.' The company of course means 'produce', rather than the 'invent' required to rhyme, but it makes the point: invention without production, distribution and consumption—without innovation, without use—is null and void for our purposes. The economic historian, then, has to investigate not so much past scientific enquiry or technical tinkering as the productive employment of what was discovered. That demanded a wider investment response. The factors impeding investment in new methods and the circumstances under which they were eventually demolished become central, as they do to the study of growth as a whole.

Even when invention was followed by innovation, much of it remained unproductive in any relevant sense. Technical change was directed towards military equipment, defence works, religious structures and buildings for display. Look at the Seven Wonders of the World: only the Pharos of Alexandria seems useful. In other words, much of the innovation that took place was induced innovation, responding to the demands of ruling elites and the state. The major exception seems to have been agriculture, where more productive change took place than has been noticed. Historians show slight interest in agriculture and admittedly the evidence is hard to handle. Although the biological changes required by farming will have cumulated in the inventory of crop and animal species entering the modern period, these things left few remains attributable to each successive era. Inferentially, nevertheless, there was a great deal of development in farming and because that sector was dominant in early economies the exception is important. It is not however quite weighty enough to disguise the fact that much pre-modern technical change was unproductive.

Full-blown growth remained rare. This is no reason to suppose that an impulse towards growth was not present: how else to explain the persistent economic expansion of the world? Rather, the forces acting against a translation of the impulse into per capita growth were strong. This applies to more than technical change. For instance when the constraints on market activity were removed markets could expand at a stunning rate. As Ernest Gellner says, many societies learn market behaviour with alacrity, once circumstances permit this or encourage it: '. . . single-end rationality may not be quite such a difficult accomplishment' (1988: 175).

Once we countenance this heterodox view of the past, with mutable processes and subterranean forces for growth working away, the significant issues before us change. They become, firstly, what forces were suppressing the growth tendency, and second what removed the negative forces in those successful cases that we do observe. In turning in these directions we may seem to grant more credit to economic success in past societies than their ingenuity actually produced. Small, isolated tribal societies indeed do seem to have offered too little scope by way of individualism or market opportunity and too much scope for social control. They lacked competitive stimulus and were prone to perpetuate the mediocrity for which Hallpike (1986) has stigmatised them.

On the other hand, larger societies offered much more scope. Their markets were potentially vast and they have a recorded history of technical innovation and diffusion, slow only by very modern standards. Structural change can be detected on occasion. A spillover into raising incomes per head was within the bounds of possibility. This is demonstrated in a recent paper by S.R.H. Jones (1988) on the way King Alfred and his children ended the cramping of growth in ninth- and tenth-century Wessex. That author's inclination is to stress the positive forces, the royal creation of public goods, in particular orderly markets. My own view is that the these goods, although important, were secondary. They were provided after the key circumstances had arisen and the key decision had been taken, to wit that the worst arbitrariness was over and would not lightly be reintroduced. What came first was the discovery by rulers that military competition could best be met from a strong market base. The economic activity of their subjects was to be fostered and gently milked, not crudely exploited. Although it was always the exception, other rulers throughout history occasionally made a similar discovery.

Was it this that was responsible for releasing *intensive* growth under premodern conditions? I think it was but there are other candidates than arbitrariness for suppressing the emergence of *intensive* growth. Besides politics designed to slice up the existing pies rather than help bake new and bigger ones, the literatures of economic history and economic development reveal a list of other features that we may suspect were responsible for suppressing *intensive* growth, such as natural resource inadequacies, hostile cultures, and inimical systems of values.

Resource difficulties we can deal with rather summarily. Resources are functions of technology. The classic illustration concerns oil and the Red Indians who could use only dribbles for cosmetics and medicine. For them it was no resource at all, not in the sense that societies able to produce lamps and engines made it a resource. Resource endowments are admittedly not totally inert. They do affect the relative costs of operating economies under any given system of technology. But neither the animating spark, nor by the same token the wet blanket that could stifle it, is to be found here. In any case, the economist would insist that trade is a substitute for resources.[3] What is needed is an explanation of variations in the rate of technical change, not of differences in resource endowment.

Cultural explanations which refer to the special privilege or talent of particular peoples are also unsatisfactory. The frequent attempts at explanation of zero *intensive* growth in terms of supposed constants such as Confucianism cannot account, say, for both income growth in Sung times and its apparent overall lack under the Ming. Neither does a common Confucian heritage sit well with the divergent economic performance of mainland and overseas Chinese during the first half of this century. At the very least something else must have mediated any Confucian effect. Shifts in the external context do seem to modify the practical content and operation of value systems in general. Alfred Marshall was especially perceptive about the way in which custom can be hollowed out by changing circumstances, its content remoulded inside an antique dress. Ceaseless adjustments take place, even as to which precepts from the bodies of didactic or religious writings are selected to rationalise practice, though as Kuran (1988) has recently pointed out, most theories of cultural conservatism overlook the feedback from actual choices to preferences. The theory of cognitive dissonance is one attempt to explain how events may modify beliefs. No doubt reasonable people will find that reality involves an interaction. Yet that would be quite different from the vastly influential Weberian style of approach in which beliefs are autonomous and it is they which drive history by causing people to modify their actions.

When cultural institutions and values do not seem to change, this may reflect the weakness of the stimuli rather than their immovability. They are in any case capable of displaying more than one face, according to circumstance, as was shown by Albert Hirschman (1985) with respect to the extended family. Whereas Western commentators for a long time regarded extended families as depressing thrift and effort, many in the Third World knew better and accepted them as low-cost co-operative forms of the firm.

The primary trick in bringing about growth thus arguably lay outside

either resource constraints or cultural rigidity. It lay in the removal of
political disincentives. This is different from growth brought about by
the positive institutional creations of the state: at least in modern times
the speed of the market response to the lifting of restraints de-
emphasises the importance of detailed debate about policy mixes. Such
debate goes on, endlessly, but it does not necessarily tell us much about
what causes growth, only about its form and who stands to win or lose
from it. These are noteworthy but secondary, almost derivative, matters.
Possible support for this opinion is to be found in the astounding rates
of growth achieved during the 1980s in mainland China, in a number
of the large coastal provinces such as Guangdong and Jiangsu, right
from the moment that restrictions on market activity were lifted. Barring
accidents we may expect to see a further spread of *intensive* growth to
countries that do not impede its emergence. This spread could be faster
than ever before because of developments in a proximate cause of
change, the transfer of advanced technologies and management techniques. As Peter Drucker (1987) observes, these things have been and
can be taught.

3. The Role of the State

We may be able to throw some light on whether the centralised
provision of public goods was indispensable for *intensive* growth by
considering whether an effective state is a necessary condition for the
presence of operating markets. A brace of tentative examples suggests
not. While they do not prove that *intensive* growth would automatically
follow without centralised provision, they do caution against assuming
that it would not. With better examples it would be useful to distinguish
between freely-operating and expanding product markets on the one
hand and markets in factors of production on the other. What is
probably crucial is the removal of command interferences, especially in
factor markets. It is political intervention by the command sector that
most requires political surgery and factor markets that most need to be
flexible. The constraints of mere custom on the other hand look
adamantine but are surprisingly responsive to economic incentives or
disincentives. This could alter the most basic aspects of social behaviour.
Sir Henry Maine pointed out that both the Spartan and Venetian
aristocracies—the latter as recently as the early eighteenth century

AD—responded to the taxing of separate households, which were deemed to come into being with separate marriages, by turning to the polyandry of brothers. In other words brothers shared a wife and saved on tax (Maine, 1883: 124). How much more responsive can custom become?

The particular cases to which we may refer where governmental provision was absent or weak relate, first, to the spontaneously crime-free trade of Dobbo in the Aru Islands, Indonesia, during the nineteenth century. 'It puts strange thoughts into one's head,' wrote Alfred Russel Wallace (1962: 336), 'about the mountain-load of government under which people exist in Europe' and, though requiring more investigation, seems to confirm that commerce was possible without governmental provision of law and order. Secondly, Gellner (1988: 233) refers to the 'astonishing' case of the Lebanon, where the level of production and economic activity remained greater, at least for some time, than in many developing societies with 'relatively effective' states. (We should point out that the states in many developing countries are probably not as strong as Gellner implies. Especially in Africa they are facades for patrimonial regimes—see Jackson, 1987). There may be an asymmetry. On the one hand a collapse of the state may, but need not, lead to a collapse of the economy, while on the other hand there may be little chance of thriving economic activity where no functioning state has ever existed. Even so, the case of Dobbo challenges the indispensability of statehood, though perhaps only for small societies.

Historically, what happened was the unintended rather than deliberate dissolution of suppressants. Unintended consequences have always been a concern of the economist: here is another set. Rather than the moment of growth's inception—a fuzzy concept in a world with prior technical change and investment growth—being what was determined by the removal of suppressants, it was growth's form that was affected. Form and pace differed so much from country to country and rested so much on positive actions that they certainly do imply complex causes for growth. But this is a little illusory. The growth impulse was there, protean yet basic, waiting to be released. It was rather the form of each country's impediments; the political processes; and the diverse channels into which growth could run, that were so complex.

Positive actions by government came only after the emergence of growth and rulers had learned that it was good. Some such measures had of course always been undertaken. Part of the task of kingship included building ever-normal granaries, unifying the coinage, and establishing courts of law. The *extensive* growth which was required to keep pace with the growth of population had itself often been accompanied by public investment. The aim was however seldom more than stabilisation or expansion, retaining the existing hierarchies and customary levels of income. Rulers and ruling elites saw no merit in actions that might cause structural change. Why should they, when it must damage their own *relative* income position?

The conscious promotion of growth was thus not usual in the premodern state. At any rate it was not primary. It followed rather than led. A government that undertook deliberate policies to encourage *intensive* growth would already be dismantling restrictions; or if market growth were occurring willy-nilly, the state would already have become too weak to maintain complete control over its subordinates.

The Bakufu—the central government—in late Tokugawa Japan is an illustration. The formidable stare on its face was belied by the reality in the provinces. Kunio (1986: 91) goes so far as to say of the provincial *han* administrative units that, 'in a sense, Tokugawa Japan consisted of some 270 autonomous states.' This decentralisation would increase the number of a government's subjects who pressed it to favour growth, to remove what were seen as major remaining obstacles. A very interesting list of what these were in the eyes of a contemporary occurs in the writings of Honda Toshiaki (Keene, 1969). The slow spiralling of change and complicated feedbacks, inscribed only on the handful of confetti which remains as documentary evidence, makes it hard to distinguish cause from effect. The Tokugawa Bakufu, when it found itself presiding over *intensive* growth, nevertheless did retain a degree of real power. The *han*s were not fully autonomous, there was some central economic policy. In the brutal circus of premodern politics these nice but uncomprehended states of balance between collapsing constraints and acts of state, between central control and local development, could survive only fortuitously. That is why they were so rare.

Despite Perry Anderson's remark (1974b: 404) that pre-capitalist social formations were more various than those of capitalism, they had in common strikingly unequal distributions of wealth, income and power. In the modern Western world power may flow from wealth; in the pre-modern world wealth flowed from power. Premodern politics were redistributive but redistributive upwards. For all the variety of political institutions, which does make the evolution of each unit a tangled tale, premodern history was very much *plus ça change, plus c'est la même chose.*

The difficulties of raising average income because of initially weak technologies, feeble institutions, and environments of high natural risk were real. It is not the intention to discount them. There was added however a more central disability: political power based on unchecked violence or the unconstrained threat of violence, which raised the social risks facing the entrepreneur. High and arbitrary taxation, even con- fiscation, was a powerful disincentive and the probability of penalties for conspicuous success even more so. Agreed, not everyone was dissuaded from taking up the profession of 'mere merchant'—the Tudor phrase for one who specialised in trade without engaging in production. Certainly there were merchants, very skilled ones, yet the total volume of commercial activity was low, particularly in the bulk carriage of utilitarian goods. Merchants existed and could be rich but they were socially and politically marginalised in most warrior societies, indeed they were often communities of outlanders. They remained peculiarly vulnerable to arbitrary treatment. The producers of manufactures were more vulnerable still. They had at risk premises, stocks of raw materials, finished goods, coin and personal wealth.

Characteristic premodern political behaviour was rent-seeking or pie-slicing, congealed though this might be into apparently static forms. The ruler and elite took by force or the threat of force a far bigger share of the social product than they contributed. The rules of government given to his son by a reportedly benevolent king of Kashmir included the injunction never to allow villagers to retain more food than they needed for one year plus the seed for the next harvest, lest they 'become in a single year very formidable . . . strong enough to neglect the commands of the king' (Singh, 1968: 39). The founder of the Tokugawa dynasty, Ieyasu, certainly set out with the intention that the peasants should 'neither live nor die' (Kunio, 1986: 92). Taxation unaccompanied by any significant return in services was the norm. Most tax was levied from the peasantry whose frequent revolts failed to force a lasting change.

The very rarity of the occasions when productive forces bore a heavy crop of fruit shows that the circumstances had to be privileged. The precise politics that let growth filter up are not yet clear. Essentially what happened was that power blocs came to cancel one another out while retaining the appearance of solidity. Ruler and nobility had to neutralise one another for enough investment income to be left in the hands of producers. We cannot specify the shares involved, nor measure them given the sources that survive, but it is obvious that this was a strait and narrow passage. Normally those with non-market power—ruler and elite—either fell out drastically, or were invaded by their peers from elsewhere, so that the impulses towards *intensive* growth were checked again.

4. The Patterns of Growth

Scholars will eventually find more cases which were successful for a time. Yet in the circumstances it is hardly surprising that we know of few noteworthy ones, among which, to repeat, Sung China, Tokugawa Japan, and early modern Europe, are outstanding. From the time of the collapse of the Sung, most of mainland Asia and the Near and Middle East was ruled by the Mongols. After their retreat there was a pause, but soon conquest regimes of similarly paralysing selfishness once more took over the main societies: the Ottomans, the Mughals, the Manchu. All suppressed or failed to tolerate *intensive* growth. Invasions by warrior hordes bent on creating exploitative empires are more definitely negative forces than the myriad possible innovations of the industrial revolution period are positive ones.

In early modern times it was some of the peripheral societies of Eurasia that underwent transitions to *intensive* growth. In them, unusual political circumstances let markets expand, entrepreneurs prosper, and growth filter up. It helped that by then enough technical knowledge had accumulated to magnify the process and keep it going. Finally, states themselves learned the advantages of assisting growth. Something of this kind happened not only in Europe but as part of the rebirth of *intensive* growth in East Asia, led this time by Japan rather than China. The world did not have to wait for a single-country industrial revolution to taste the fruits of *intensive* growth.

Chapter Four

Ecological Regimes and The Rise of Organised Religion

Johan Goudsblom

This chapter and the following one, on 'Military-Agrarian Regimes', belong together. They both deal, in a highly general way, with the origins of contemporary institutions—of organised religion and war, and the social hierarchies associated with these institutions.

I have tried to follow a consistently 'processual' approach as outlined in the introductory paper and to see how this may be applied to the emergence of ruling classes of priests and warriors in agrarian societies. As the scope of my survey is very large, what I have to say is exploratory rather than conclusive. This is a personal inquiry, not a summary of 'the state of the art'. Its purpose is to bring together pieces of information gathered from various fields and to see how they may be fitted into a coherent perspective. As my guiding principle I have used the idea that nothing is ever self-evident and there is always room for inquiring into how things have become what they now are.[1]

1. Religion and Social Process

In the case of religion this principle is incompatible with the widely held belief that religions may change but religion as such is eternal. In anthropology, this belief found expression more than a hundred years ago in Edward Tylor's theory of stages according to which mankind, since its earliest origins, had passed through successive stages of religious evolution—from animism through polytheism to monotheism. Religion became as it were increasingly more 'civilised'; but 'man' was religious from the start: *Homo religiosus* appeared to be ageless.[2]

Along the same lines it could be argued that 'man' is belligerent by nature; that there is an equally timeless *Homo bellicosus*, and that war, like religion, is inherent in the human condition.

In this and the following paper, I shall allow myself the freedom to doubt these postulates and, instead, to entertain the hypothesis that religion and war have been the result of particular socio-cultural processes in human history. We have words in our languages such as 'secularisation' and 'pacification' which point to movements in the opposite direction: away from religion and war. Is it not equally possible that these counter-movements were preceded by trends *towards* religion and war—by 'religification' and 'martialisation' or 'bellification'?

I shall not advocate that we enrich our vocabulary with these neologisms. I only mention them in order to suggest that neither a state of war nor a state of religion need be the 'natural' state for human beings to be in.

My research on the domestication of fire has only strengthened my distrust of regarding any social institution as eternal and universal.[3] The domestication of fire is a process which has been going on for hundreds of thousands of years. Studying it has imbued me with a sense of the enormous continuity of human culture: human groups have transmitted the skill of keeping a fire for many thousands of generations. Nevertheless, there *was* a time when human groups did not have fire. So, while there is impressive continuity, this does not imply timelessness.

Similarly, the social institutions and mental attitudes which we nowadays associate with 'religion' may also be less universal and less ancient than we are generally taught to assume. As I shall try to show, a strong case can be made for the hypothesis that these institutions and attitudes first took shape only some 300 to 500 generations ago, after the emergence of agriculture.

2. Religion and the Rise of Agriculture

As I argued in Chapter 1, wherever the process of agrarianisation gained momentum, a cluster of five closely interrelated trends tended to become dominant:

1. towards an increase in food, and an increase in people;
2. towards greater concentrations of food, and greater concentrations of people;
3. towards an increasing specialisation in the production and consumption of food, and an increasing specialisation of people;
4. towards an increase in organisations allocating food and coordinating people over longer distances;
5. towards an increasing differentiation of power or 'stratification' among people.

Of most interest to us at present are the third and the fifth trend, specialisation and stratification. We can observe that wherever the size and density of population increased, people also became increasingly differentiated according to their occupation and, concomitantly, their rank, class or caste. Generally speaking, four major categories emerged: peasants, artisans, priests, and warriors.

This is, of course, a very rough classification. The distinctions are not always perfectly clear and many overlapping cases may be discerned: peasants who were also artisans, artisans who were also priests, and so on. Charting all the historical varieties, however, is not my concern here. I maintain that, by and large, the four-fold classification is valid and can be applied to a great number of empirical cases.

The question then arises of how this general pattern is to be explained. It is not difficult to account for the fact that the bulk of the population consisted of peasants working the land; nor do we need to stretch our imagination to understand the emergence of craftsmen and traders. The matter becomes intriguing, however, when we turn to the formation of special classes of priests and warriors, and their rise to social dominance. In this chapter I shall focus upon the priests. The problem is, then, how in societies composed of farmers or peasants (who themselves stemmed from foragers, from gatherers and hunters) a new group of specialists, the priests, could emerge—the upper crust of which subsequently could establish itself (along with, and in rivalry with, warrior elites) as a ruling class for many centuries.[4]

Such a fundamental change as the formation of a 'new class' can only be explained by relating it to other changes. It makes no sense to try to infer the rise to power of either priests or warriors from an unchanging image of 'man' as a creature that has been always by nature religious and belligerent, a *Homo religiosus* and a *Homo bellicosus*. Obviously, if 'man' were incapable of religion and war, neither priests nor warriors would ever have come upon the stage. But then the same could be said about space travel and so many other things.

Emphasising process and change does not mean, however, that I wish to deny continuity. There is a great deal of continuity between pre-agrarian and agrarian societies: the control of fire, which has been an essential precondition for agriculture, is a case in point. It represents a socially acquired skill—an element of culture in the sense of being 'learned, shared and transmitted'[5]—that has been handed down from generation to generation since the Lower Palæolithic. Then, in the Upper Palæolithic, 'broad spectrum economies' developed which in their highly advanced techniques of hunting and gathering as well as of storing and preserving food already anticipated pastoralism and agriculture in many ways (see Wenke, 1984: 155–69).

In spite of the strong underlying continuities the emergence of agrarian societies, using domesticated plants and animals, heralded a new stage in human social evolution and history. And it was in these agrarian societies that priests gradually came into their own as a separate and distinct class, with their specific modes of dress, habits, and professional secrets. In the European Middle Ages, the clergy adorned itself with the title 'First Estate'. This may not any longer have reflected the actual power relations; but it did correspond with the fact that, from a historical point of view, the priests probably *were* the first estate. If we can speak of an 'oldest profession', it may well be that of priesthood.[6] (Incidentally, the very word that we still use to indicate a rank order of established authority is 'hierarchy'—which literally means 'holy rule', 'rule by priests'.)

It may even be due to the long-standing influence of priests that the problem of the social origins—the sociogenesis—of the office and authority of priests is seldom raised. After all, viewed from a priestly tradition itself this question is pointless, for the institution of priesthood as a First Estate or Highest Caste is regarded as a divine and timeless arrangement which does not need to be explained in sociological or sociogenetic terms at all.

3. The Persistence of Theological Reasoning

Interestingly, this theological train of thought still resounds in most scholarly writing about religion and priests today—even by authors who would not hesitate to regard their own approach as thoroughly secular. It is quite common to say that the priests fulfil a 'mediating role' between human beings and 'the spirit world' or 'the supernatural' or 'the gods'. I could fill the rest of this paper with quotations illustrating this way of writing about priests.[7] I shall restrict myself to a small selection from a book on the doctrine of the Three Orders or Three Estates in medieval Europe by the French historian, Georges Duby. 'The bishop', he writes, 'was a sacred personage, a Christ, the Lord's Anointed; passing through his skin, mixing with, penetrating his entire body, the chrism impregnated him forever with divine power'. . . . 'Anointment', Duby continues, 'brought with it another gift: *sapientia*, a gaze capable of penetrating behind the veil of appearances to reach hidden truths. Only the bishop possessed the keys to the truth.' Or, in other words, 'Anointment had placed the bishop right at the point where heaven and earth were joined, between the visible and the invisible.' . . . 'Because of his median, intermediary position, the bishop bore a special obligation to contribute to the harmony between the two worlds, that essential concord which Satan strove ceaselessly to disrupt' (Duby: 1980: 14–15).

Clearly, these words carry a theological ring. Anthropologists might say that Duby is giving an 'emic' description: he puts himself into the frame of mind of the medieval bishops themselves to such an extent that he is actually only paraphrasing the doctrine they propounded *in their own terms*; until, rather suddenly, he switches to an 'etic' idiom, as he concludes: 'In the Carolingian tradition, the episcopate was by nature the producer of ideology' (Duby, 1980: 16).

I must admit that I find all this somewhat unsatisfactory and, frankly speaking, a bit too easy. If we take Duby literally, there was a god, there were people, laymen, and the bishop's authority rested on the fact that he mediated between these two parties. Or maybe we should interpret Duby's words more liberally, as if he is actually saying: 'there was a religion, a belief, and according to this belief the bishop played a mediating role'. But even then the question remains why all the other people were willing to accept a set of beliefs that was so obviously to the bishop's advantage.

Again, instead of Duby I could have chosen many other examples. This is the customary way in which historians, anthropologists and sociologists write about religion and priests. One other example can serve as a stepping-stone to my further argument. It is a description of temple ceremonies in ancient Mesopotamia by the archaeologist, Seton Lloyd, whose expert knowledge I do not doubt for a moment. But note the words he has chosen:

> High amongst the services which the gods required of their worshippers was the provision of food, drink, and oil for annointing. According to H.W.F. Saggs, 'The gods enjoyed regular meals . . . which were deposited upon tables before the divine images.' Their food included bread in large quantities, the meat of sheep or cattle and drink in the form of beer, which was greatly favoured by the Sumerians. Among provisions listed in later times were honey, ghee, fine oil, milk, dates, figs, salt, cakes, poultry, fish and vegetables.

For those who still might wonder after reading this extensive menu how it was actually consumed by the gods, the description is followed by a brief explanation in small print:

> The meal of the gods was technically a banquet to which other deities [?] were invited and at which the human worshippers and even the dead [?] might be present. The gods themselves received special parts of the animals, the remainder going to the king, the priests and the temple staff. (Lloyd, 1984: 44)

In the last sentence, I think, we get a glimpse of what actually went on during these temple feasts. The ceremonies were held in honour of the gods, but these gods (that is to say, their images) were only provided with 'special parts' of the meat; the rest went 'to the king, the priests, and the temple staff'.

I suggest that instead of writing that the meals were served to the gods it might be more straightforward to state that they were intended for a group of men, mainly priests.

In this respect, something might be learned from the texts of ancient Judaism, which could be surprisingly candid on this score. I am not directly referring to such anecdotes as the one in the Book of Daniel which tells us how the priests of Bel in Babylon used to let themselves secretly into the temple at night to indulge in the food that had been sacrificed at the altar during the day—a piece of gossip revealing how the adherents of different religions regarded each other's ceremonies (*Daniel*, 14: 1–22). More interesting in our present context is the wealth of information in the opening chapters of Leviticus about the proceedings in the service of the Jewish religion itself and about the portions of various sacrifices to which the priests were entitled. Leviticus lists various types of offerings: burnt offerings, meat offerings, sin offerings, trespass offerings, consecrations, and peace offerings. Each type of sacrifice had its own rules; in some, the whole animal was burnt, as 'an offering made by fire, of a sweet savour unto the Lord', whereas in others, only a few stipulated parts were burnt and the remainder was allocated to the priests. They, and they alone, should eat it, 'for it is most holy'; no lay person was allowed to touch it: if anything was still left over on the third day, that 'shall bè burnt with fire' (*Lev.* 7: 5, 17).

Not all the priests of Israel appear to have been as particular about these rules. Here is what the first Book of Samuel has to say about the sons of the priest Eli who worked for their father in the temple of Shiloh:

Now the sons of Eli were sons of Belial; they knew not of the Lord. And the priests' custom with the people was, that, when any man offered sacrifice, the priest's servant came, while the flesh was in seething, with a fleshhook of three teeth in his hand. And he struck it into the pan, or kettle, or cauldron, or pot; all that the fleshhook brought up the priest took for himself. So they did in Shiloh unto all the Israelites that came there. Also before they burnt the fat, the priest's servant came to the man that sacrificed. Give flesh to roast for the priest; for he will not have sodden flesh of thee, but raw. And if any man said to him, Let them not fail to burn the fat presently, and then take as much as thy soul desireth; then he would answer him, Nay; but thou shalt give it to me now; and if not, I will take it by force. Wherefore the sin of the young men was very great before the Lord; for men abhorred the offering of the Lord'. (1 *Sam.* 2: 12–17)

This story clearly exposes abuse of the priestly office. It also shows us something of the balance of power between the priests who controlled the altar and the ordinary people who came to it with their offerings. Apparently the priests took in food and possibly other revenues as well; in this respect they were at the receiving end. What did they do in exchange which made the other people willing to support them?

With regard to any form of regularly recurring social behaviour we may safely assume, I think, that (unless the power balance is very uneven) it fulfils certain functions for the various people involved. In the case of the sons of Eli it is not difficult to see some of the functions the rites of sacrifice had for *them*; the intriguing question is what functions the rites had for those who came to offer their meat and their bread?

Obviously the scope of this question is by no means restricted to ancient Israel. In a great many other agrarian societies, past and present, similar arrangements prevailed, with priests being able to support themselves through the gifts of others. What precisely was the nature of the social service they provided in return?

4. The Rise of Agrarian Regimes

Agrarian societies, regardless of their many varieties, have one common feature in which they differ significantly from the far more ancient type of foraging society in which people had been living for thousands of generations. They are both more productive and more vulnerable.

Agriculture involves deliberate intervention by human groups in the blind process of natural selection between and within species. It involves sustained attempts at eliminating the growth of unwanted plants from a field and fostering the growth of wanted plants—primarily those known to be edible. The effort required is known as work; the result, if successful, is increased productivity.

Note that this is a sociological way of conceiving of productivity. Economists—and many anthropologists who have dealt with this issue as well—tend to define productivity as output per man-hour.[8] This individual-centred definition leads to the conclusion that foraging societies were more productive than agrarian societies, for people did not have to work as hard. Such a conclusion is misleading, however, in that it diverts our attention from the undeniable fact that on the whole, as collectivities, agrarian societies produced greater quantities of food than gatherers and hunters ever did.

This fact had far-reaching consequences. Because the land they worked yielded more products that were useful to them and fewer that were useless, increasing numbers of people could find subsistence in a given area. Whenever, as a result, the population increased, it grew more dependent upon the very products of agriculture. There were more mouths to be fed, while the 'wild' terrain suitable for gathering and hunting diminished. Consequently, the only resources left for people were their crops and their livestock, and this state of one-sided dependency made them especially vulnerable.

Three types of danger with which people always had to cope became all the more threatening to agrarian communities. The types of danger I am referring to form a triad, corresponding to what Norbert Elias has called a 'triad of basic controls' (1970: 156–7). First, there were the many dangers that came from the non-human, or *extra-human*, world: droughts or, the opposite, rains and floods; parasites; weeds; exhaustion of the soil. Secondly, there were the dangers emanating from *inter-human* relations: the always-lurking chance that hostile groups of humans would pillage and destroy the crops and the stores. And then, thirdly, there was the risk that the harvest would fail or be lost through faulty sowing, nursing, harvesting or storing—in other words through mismanagement due to *intra-human* nature: to negligence, ignorance or greed, to lack of care, discipline or foresight.

The threefold classification of extra-, inter- and intra-human dangers may help us, I think, to explain the emergence of priests and warriors in agrarian societies, including the sequence in which they emerged. (The issue of sequence is only secondary, however, to my main thesis regarding the sociogenesis of priestly and warrior groups as such.)

During the first stages of agriculture the dangers of predation and plunder by other human groups were relatively small; there was not much to steal, and there were few potential robbers around. All the greater, however, were the dangers involved in the extra-human forces of nature that could ruin a harvest, and in the intra-human inclination toward laziness and self-indulgence that could have equally devastating effects.

Although some of us today may be inclined to view the life of farmers or peasants in pre-industrial societies as standing 'close to nature', cultivating crops is certainly not something inborn that is given to humanity 'by nature'. Everything about it has to be learned and it poses problems which can only be handled with the aid of elaborate socio-cultural arrangements.

Paramount among the problems with which the early agriculturalists had to cope was, of course, the question of how to deal with the plants and animals they were trying to 'domesticate'. The process of domestication implied that groups of people entered into a new symbiosis with some specially favoured species which they had originally encountered in the wild, which they now began to take under their own care, and which they tried to subject to an ecological regime controlled by themselves.

In order to establish this regime people had to have knowledge of the plants and animals and of the conditions furthering or impeding their growth. They needed, in other words, knowledge of 'extra-human nature'. The evidence suggests that this was an area in which priests claimed—and to some extent also possessed—expertise. When in the literature mention is made of the 'mediating role' that priests fulfilled between the ordinary people and the 'supernatural', the authors usually are referring to some sort of competence—real or alleged—in dealing with problems regarding the weather and the seasons, or parasites and pests.

Thus priests often took upon themselves the task of 'timing'. It was—and still is—of vital interest for farmers to know when the moment had come to till the land, to sow, to weed, to harvest, to break into the winter stocks. If they started sowing or planting too early, the young seedlings might freeze or be washed away by a torrent of rain; postponing the sowing too long would mean, on the other hand, that precious days of growth would be lost and weeds could sprout too easily. Harvesting raised similar problems: if done too soon, one would miss the chance of further ripening, if done too late, the crops might be exposed to rain or frost.

Human beings are not equipped with a 'biogram' for agrarian life. They have no innate calendar telling them when the time is ripe for preparing the soil, for planting the seeds, for removing weeds, for harvesting. The only calendar available to people is a socio-cultural one: among the tasks with which priests in agrarian societies used to be entrusted was the management of the calendar. They had to register, by observing the position of sun, moon and stars, whether the time had come for certain agrarian activities.

Orientation was not all, however. In his book *Time: an Essay*—so far unfortunately published only in German and Dutch—Norbert Elias quotes from the memoirs of an old Krobo man (the Krobo are a tribe living in what is now Ghana) describing how in the olden days the priest used to determine the moment when the farmers had to go out and sow their wheat. In order to do so he would climb the mountain at the centre of the Krobo territory every morning to observe the sunrise. Once the sun made its first appearance behind a certain rock, the priest would shout a signal which resounded all over the mountain, and then 'you could see the farmers and their families running down the mountain with their baskets and hoes to get to work' (Elias, 1984: 16–17).

Even if the informant quoted by Elias may have drawn a slightly idealised picture of the ritual—which he had never witnessed himself, because it had already died out before he was a child—his description remains valuable as an account of the functions attributed to priests. Another detail is also worth noting: people were allowed to repeat the priest's signal, a magical formula, while they were sowing; but if anyone dared to do so later, after the sowing was done, he would be punished severely and 'he might even be sent away in slavery.

This piece of information clearly brings out that the agrarian regime was not just a regime over plants and animals but also over people.[9] As a regime over people it consisted, to use Elias's terms, in part of external constraints and in part of—complementary—self-restraints. Priests played a prominent part in it; and they were able to do so, I think, because their task was vitally important for the entire community—not only because of the orientation they provided but, perhaps even more so, because of the discipline they exerted. The discipline could be binding, even if the grounds on which the priests based their decisions appeared to be unfathomable and arbitrary. In uncertain situations a randomly given directive would at least bring the relief that someone was prepared to assume responsibility.

Again, I do not wish to suggest that the problems with which farmers had to cope were altogether new, and had never bothered gatherers and hunters. My point is that as agrarian communities grew in size and density some problems became particularly acute and could only be met through special forms of discipline. I am thinking of the need to *work* hard in order to produce food; the need to *store* stocks of food and seed for a considerable time; and the need to *distribute* these stocks among the members of the community in a fair and satisfactory way.

In a series of thought-provoking papers and books the anthropologist Marvin Harris (1974, 1977, 1985, 1988) has turned our attention to the fact that in agrarian communities the problems of preserving and distributing food were no less compelling than those of producing it. In order to be able to survive periods of scarcity, these communities would have to attain a level of production exceeding their immediate needs in normal times. Such abundance might ordinarily not seem necessary in the short term, but in the longer run, as a buffer against unforeseen exigencies, it was. I would argue that rites conducted by priests helped to strengthen the self-restraint which could keep people from too readily drawing upon their reserves.

Think once more of the Old Testament, which to many of us is the most familiar source about life under a strict agrarian regime. The teachings it contains are typically directed to people who every day found themselves confronted with the sort of problems I have just mentioned. They had to earn their bread by the sweat of their brow; they had to be thrifty; and they had to see to it that no one among their own kin suffered need—for the presence of people living in destitution could form a serious menace to a small farming community. Diligence, frugality, and a sense of social responsibility—these were the prime virtues. And admonitions to live up to them were accompanied by the endlessly repeated call to obedience to God: one always had to observe one's religious duties and do honour to the priests.

It should be clear that although I keep referring to the Bible my argument is couched in a developmental rather than a biblical train of thought. I observe that the great majority of agrarian societies in the past had priests; this leads me to the question of which (socially formed) needs the priests met or, in other words, which functions they fulfilled that could serve to explain their prominent position. I am even prepared to argue that, at a certain stage of agrarian development, societies *with* priests had greater chances of survival than societies *without* priests.

The functions of priests, in my view, included both orientation and discipline—with regard to work and production, and also with regard to problems of storing and distributing, of preservation and con-sumption. I particularly wish to stress that the latter problems were at least as important as those of work and production. A successful harvest brought in at a single time a far greater quantity of food than foragers could ever collect—more, too, than the best catch of the hunters of large game. This harvest would be the main subsistence for the entire community for many months to come. All this raised unprecedented problems, constituting many potential sources of uncertainty and conflict. The priests, I would argue, offered binding solutions to these problems in the form of rites. These rites, to be performed by themselves or under their direction, were standard ways of coping with the problems arising from the social conditions in which the farmers found themselves living.

As I pointed out, these problems had to do with external, extra-human as well as with internal, intra-human nature. For a harvest to be successful, people always remained dependent upon sun, wind, and rain—natural forces over which they could exert no control but to which they could try to adjust themselves to the best of their knowledge. What Calvinist theologians later were to say about divine grace also applied to a successful harvest: even if you did your best, you could never be sure that the outcome would be good; but if you failed to do your best, a bad outcome would certainly lie ahead of you. Priests, I think, helped to impress this insight upon people and to make them live in accordance with it, so that, for the sake of a harvest which would always remain uncertain, they would be willing to summon the patience and the industry without which the crops were bound to fail.

This was not all. Even if a rich harvest were reaped, the community had not nearly come to the end of its problems. On the contrary, it was put to the test once more. How could some—the strongest—members of the community be prevented from seizing the sudden plenitude and appropriating the best parts of it, or worst of all feasting on it until nothing remained, neither food nor seed-corn?

The problems of preservation and distribution were all the more pressing since greed tends to be contagious. If a few members of a group helped themselves too eagerly from the supplies, others could hardly afford to lag behind. Whoever failed to join in would appear to harm himself and his own. How, then, could this vicious circle be broken?

It was broken, I think, by an invention that was as simple as it was ingenious and the importance of which can hardly be overrated. A social institution was developed which offset both the individual inclination towards greed in the face of sudden abundance and the social mechanism of contagion triggered by it. The institution I have in mind was that of harvest feasts. During a brief period, the community was allowed to feast collectively on the crops; but after a few days the feast was called to an end and frugal times began again. The feasts were led by the priests. They were also the ones to terminate the feasting.

The pressures of frugality under which agriculturalists lived rested even more heavily upon those (and they were the majority) who combined agriculture with pastoralism. In addition to their stores of crops they also had, so to speak, an excellent supply of meat permanently at hand. The temptation to kill an animal in times of adversity was therefore always present. What could be more effective to counter this temptation than making slaughter into a strictly ritual activity, to be performed only by the priests or, at best, with priestly permission? Could it be purely accidental, we may well ask ourselves, that Easter happens to fall in early springtime, shortly after the tender lambs are born?

These considerations help to understand the seemingly paradoxical fact that in the rites of harvest and slaughter not only feasting but sacrifice played a central role. Making a sacrifice, so it seems, became the standard way in which people expressed their willingness to deny themselves certain immediately tempting pleasures, and to submit to a regime of renunciation, even in the midst of plenitude.

In an interesting historical and anthropological study Bruce Lincoln has compared two semi-nomadic peoples whose primary means of subsistence was cattle: the Indo-Iranians of the third and second millennia BC, and the Nilotics of Eastern Africa, many of whom are still leading a similar existence today. Among both peoples slaughtering cattle was strictly forbidden, unless it were done by priests. Among the Dinka in Eastern Africa, Lincoln (1981: 44) writes, 'no man will take it upon himself to kill so valuable and beloved an animal as an ox or cow simply because he is hungry'; it is only as a sacrifice that an ox may be done to death. The Indo-Iranians acted no differently: in their language one and the same word apparently stood for 'domesticated animal', 'cattle', and 'sacrificial animal'; another word may be translated either as 'cattle' or as 'that which may only be killed as a sacrifice' (Lincoln, 1981: 65, 155–6).

One problem remains intriguing. In the offering rituals from Mesopotamia and ancient Israel to which I referred above, the sacrifices were made up mostly of meat, and first-rate meat at that (for in these ceremonies only the best seemed good enough and only animals without blemish were accepted). As I pointed out, considerable portions of this meat were eaten by the priests. If we are to believe the book of Leviticus, however, this was not always the case. There were occasions when the entire sacrifice, which might be a splendid bull, was burnt and sent up in smoke. How could *this* apparent waste be explained sociologically?

What chances of survival were enhanced by letting precious food go up into thin air?

This question, too, may perhaps be answered by putting it within the context of the problems of preservation and distribution. Again, a helpful clue may be found in the work of Marvin Harris, although he can be held in no way responsible for the hypothesis I am about to offer. A radical way to get rid of the problem of distributing food that has become chronically scarce, he writes, is simply to make this food forbidden for everybody—as has happened with pork among the Jews and the Muslims and with beef among the Hindus (Harris, 1977: 193–232). Both taboos are seen by Harris as the result of a long-term historical process of intensification of agriculture leading to ecological changes which made the keeping of pigs and cows increasingly costly. As a domesticated species, pigs had little more to offer than their meat, and that could be done without. Oxen and cows, on the other hand, provided the human population of India with vitally necessary services such as traction power and milk. Whereas the most ancient Vedic scriptures gave detailed instructions on how priests were to slaughter cattle, later Hindu traditions have sanctified the cow as a sacred animal, just as in the Middle Eastern religions the pig has been declared unclean.

Letting a sacrifice go up in smoke is a way of tabooing it: this is food that no one may touch any more, not even a priest. Could it be that this custom originated somewhat along the following lines? It would seem likely that in a society of pastoralists such as the Indo-Iranians people occasionally tried to evade the ban on slaughtering, and it is equally likely that some of them were caught in the act. What was to happen in such a situation? The offender would have to be punished, of course, but what was to be done with the killed animal? Since it would seem highly improper to let other people feast on it, a more drastic solution seemed called for: that of ostentatiously burning the entire animal that had been wrongly killed.

Let me make one further step on this increasingly speculative track and venture the supposition that while the sacrifice was being made the spectators at such ceremonies may have pondered to *whom* it was being made. Who might be the recipient of this delicious meat?

I do not wish to claim that the idea of gods originated exclusively in this sort of ritual; but I do think that these rituals helped to shape it. The ritualisation of slaughter and its monopolisation by the priests went hand in hand with what would now be called the 'criminalisation' of non-ritual killing, eventually resulting in its virtual elimination.

The offering rituals, like the harvest feasts, were ceremonies with strong disciplinary functions. In the long run, agricultural and pastoral groups observing such rituals stood a better chance of surviving than groups resisting such rituals. The priests, who served as the masters of the ceremonies, bolstered the rituals with ideas about a world of gods who would be the grateful (if not wrathful) receivers of the delicacies which those who brought their offerings were denying themselves. In doing so, the priests also advanced the idea that they were the intermediaries between this world in which people lived and worked and the other, 'supernatural' world, and that in this function, as intermediaries, they were indispensible.

I realise that I have ended on a very speculative note. Let me therefore briefly summarise the main points I have tried to make:

1. I have noted a tendency among historians, anthropologists and sociologists to deal with problems of religion and priesthood too readily in theological terms.

2. I have then tried to state the problem of how priests came to be a ruling group in agrarian societies as a sociological problem.

3. I have tried to find a solution by applying the concept of agrarian regime, and argued that priests fulfilled important functions in agrarian regimes, providing orientation, co-ordination and discipline.

Chapter Five

The Formation of Military-Agrarian Regimes

Johan Goudsblom

1. The Stratification of Agrarian Societies

Ever since the domestication of fire began, a steady undercurrent in the development and history of human society has been the extension of human hegemony over other species. With the emergence of agriculture and pastoralism, this trend entered a new stage, as some species (the domesticates) were now protected and brought under human control, while others (the remaining wild species) were—if not exterminated—more or less effectively kept away from the expanding human domain. Almost inevitably, the availability of more land that people could exploit exclusively for themselves and their domesticates resulted in population growth—a process to which some biologists might refer as increases in human biomass, and which Eric Jones and other economic historians would call *extensive* growth. In a few cases, moreover, an increasing supply of goods per capita, or *intensive* growth, was obtained in the long run.

Almost everywhere in the development of agrarian societies the gains that were made in material prosperity tended to be distributed very unequally over the population. In other words, increased productivity at this stage did not engender a general rise in the standard of living but resulted rather in a process of increasing social stratification—of differentiation of people according to power, property, and prestige. As noted before, the four major categories that emerged were those of peasants; craftsmen and traders; priests; and warriors. All over the world and in different historical eras, a similar fourfold division of social categories arose, with similar hierarchical implications. Regardless of the enormous variety of its specific historical guises, this was the basic pattern of stratification in a wide range of agrarian societies, from ancient Mesopotamia to pre-Columbian Mexico and Peru, from pre-industrial Britain to pre-industrial Japan, among the Celts and among the Ashanti.

In all these societies the majority of the population consisted of peasants: they tilled the soil and were at the bottom of the social hierarchy. Craftsmen and traders were far fewer in numbers. Some of them might attain considerable wealth but they rarely rose to the highest ranks. The supreme positions in the hierarchy of power, property and prestige were monopolised by priests and warriors. This is not to say that all priests and warriors were rich and powerful. Many of them were hardly better off than the poorest peasant. The point is that the ruling elites were composed of priests and warriors and—in some very advanced agrarian states—their descendants.

In the previous chapter, on ecological regimes and the rise of organised religion, I tried to explain how priests could become so powerful. Here I turn to the warriors. My explanation will run along parallel lines. It will focus, again, upon the emergence and subsequent development of agrarian regimes.

2. Agrarian regimes

Productivity and vulnerability—this combination of conditions under which peasants had to live forms, in my view, the key to understanding the common underlying power structure in advanced agrarian societies.

For societies which embarked on agrarianisation there was, in the long run, no way back—if only because increased productivity tended to lead to an increase of population and a decrease of wild territory in which people could find their subsistence by gathering and hunting.

As a consequence, peoples engaged in agriculture increasingly found themselves compelled to live under a new form of ecological regime—an agrarian regime. They simply had no choice. In the previous chapter I have sketched what was probably the oldest form of such a regime: the religious-agrarian regime, led by priests. Wherever these *religious-agrarian regimes* were established, however, they found themselves in the course of time in competition with, and had to make room for, *military-agrarian regimes*, led by warriors.

I use the term 'make room for', because this leaves open a great many possibilities, ranging from the virtual elimination of an authoritative priestly class—as in ancient Greece and Rome—to all sorts of shared dominance, such as the co-existence of 'secular' and 'spiritual' elites in medieval Europe.

To be sure, the emergence of military-agrarian regimes was a dominant, not a universal trend. There are indeed documents from societies with rather intensive agriculture in which hardly any mention is made of either priests or warriors. One such document is the didactic poem *Works and Days* by Hesiod, the Greek poet who lived around 700 B.C.[1] He begins by avowing his distaste for military strife. It is much better, he says, for people to compete in peaceful pursuits: let potters vie with potters, in skill, and bards with bards. Hesiod himself, as a bard, sings the praise of the old agrarian virtues of diligence, thrift, and social responsibility. He does so, however, without any reference to priestly guidance. Instead, he urges his listeners and readers to restrain their impulses toward idling, squandering and quarrelling *of their own accord* —because it is, after all, in their own interest. In other words, Hesiod commends an agrarian regime relying upon self-restraint, not unlike the moral regime of self-restraint that Max Weber (1904–5) described as 'the Protestant ethic'.

I shall return to Hesiod later. I have mentioned him here as representing an extreme case—a highly exceptional and intriguing deviation from the way agrarian regimes were maintained in most parts of the world most of the time.

Far more typical was the social world evoked by the other great early Greek poet, Homer. Consider the following passage from the *Odyssey*:

> The same wind as wafted me from Ilium brought me to Ismarus, the city of the Cicones. I sacked this place and destroyed the men who held it. Their wives and the rich plunder that we took from the town we divided so that no one, as far as I could help it, should go short of his proper share.[2]

Clearly, these are the words of a warrior. The narrator is Odysseus, and the casual, matter-of-fact way in which he tells us what took place when he happened to land at Ismarus gives us an impression of how he and his men used to go about during their overseas wanderings:

pillaging and plundering. But then, just like the peasants tilling their soil, they seemed to have no other choice; this was their way of making a living.

The latter may be slightly exaggerated: the Cicones had been allies of Troy, and Odysseus might have felt justified in treating them as his enemies. At the opposite pole, he might find a hospitable welcome in the palace of a friendly lord. Such a generous reception would only be given, however, on a basis of reciprocity by men of equal rank—by noblemen, wealthy and reputable warriors capable of holding their own and, if challenged, defending their honour in combat (cf. Finley, 1977).

It is interesting to compare the actions of Odysseus with those of the Krobo priest to whom I referred in the previous chapter, who would serenely climb up to his vantage point on the mountain every morning in order to watch whether the time for sowing had come. As they are portrayed in the stories that have come down to us, both Odysseus and this priest knew, each in his own way, how to command authority. They did so, however, in very different capacities: the one as the leader of military operations, the other as the leader of religious rituals. They represented almost as antipodes the two types of rule by warriors and by priests.

As I said before, we should not draw too idyllic a picture of the part played by the Krobo priest. According to the account of their chronicler the Krobos originally came from Dahomey; they had fled because they found the rule of the king of Dahomey too oppressive. While on their way they engaged in battle with other peoples; after many wanderings and conflicts they finally found a home on the heights of the Krobo mountain (Azu, 1929: 6–10; see also Huber, 1963).

The entire history, told in a few pages, is remarkably similar to the adventures of the people of Israel as told in the first books of the Old Testament. No more than the ancient Israelites did the Krobos live in a society that was free from war. However, they had managed to find refuge in an area where war was not endemic, and where the priest could assume leadership in the rituals of agrarian life. They had found relative peace for a while, beyond the reach of the military-agrarian kingdoms of West Africa. But even here they had to contend with forces which were conducive to war. Thus, our chronicler tells us, in a neighbouring tribe the chief was so belligerent that his own people, in order to stop him from drawing them all into war, chopped off his right hand (Azu, 1929: 9).

3. Intermezzo: the Reception Effect and its Implications

This anecdote raises the question of the degree to which war, or religion, is 'natural' and 'universal'. I shall diverge from my actual subject for a moment to address this question, and discuss briefly the 'reception effect'. It is very simple; everyone who has ever attended a reception is familiar with it. When the first few persons enter the room where a reception is going to be held, they can carry on a conversation in a normal voice. As more people come in to join the party, however, the volume of noise in the room increases; and in order to make themselves understood people have to continue raising their voices—thus adding more and more decibels to the general murmur. After a while everybody is speaking at the top of his voice, and nobody can really understand what the other person is saying.

Does this mean that human beings have a natural propensity for talking as loudly as they can? No. The moral of this digression is clear: it is the pressure of the social circumstances—or, to put it more learnedly, the dynamics of the social figuration they form together[3]—that makes people raise their voices. Everyone is shouting because everyone else is shouting.

A full recognition of the social mechanisms at work in the 'reception effect' is conducive to the methodological stance of taking nothing in human conduct for granted. The volume of noise produced in the reception room at any given moment can only be explained as a function of the process of 'noisification'; after a while, it has passed its peak, and 'denoisification' sets in. The same observation applies to a great many other social processes, including militarisation and pacification. There is no reason to regard a continuous state of war as the 'natural' condition for human beings to live in—nor is there any ground for making such a claim for the opposite: the ideal of paradisiac peace. The whole idea of a 'natural state' in which human beings might ever have lived is highly dubious; for in which stage of social development should such a state be situated? It seems more reasonable to take a processual view and to suppose that there have been periods in human history when peoples in certain areas could live in comparative peace, and periods when they could hardly avoid becoming entangled in violent encounters. The explanation for the varying degrees to which groups felt—and actually were—threatened by each other cannot be found in an unchanging 'human nature'. Here again the adage applies that changes can best be explained by relating them to other changes.

There is another general principle that may be illustrated by the story about the unfortunate chief who could no longer pursue his warlike ambitions because his own people had mutilated him. What this tale points to is the presence, I dare say always and everywhere, of countervailing trends. And these trends should not be conceived of as abstract, almost metaphysical forces; they are embodied in concrete human beings—some of whom (as in this case) may be primarily interested in peace, others in war. The same tendencies may, of course, operate in the same persons, who will then be torn by conflicting motives. In any case, if in a society dominant trends can be observed tending in a certain direction, we are always well advised to look for countervailing trends as well, pulling people in other directions, and to inquire why the countervailing trends were outweighed by the trends that turned out to be dominant.

4. Stages in the Monopolisation of Violence

Many societies have gone through periods—often prolonged periods—in their history during which wars were inevitable and seemed to belong to the natural order of things. This could be so even in the absence of a distinct class of warriors; in tribal societies, all the young men could be admitted to the warrior group after they had passed the proper rites of initiation. This was customary, for example, among most Indian tribes in North America, whom European missionaries described as being involved in annually recurring deadly struggles—struggles which would end in the most cruel humiliations and tortures of the vanquished.[4]

These tribal societies represented an early stage in a process that is still continuing: the monopolisation of violence by organised specialists.[5] During the first stage of this process, which extends far back into hominid prehistory, group violence increasingly became a prerogative of men. Of course, women and children could never be completely kept from using physical force amongst each other and even against men, but they tended to be excluded from organised fights between groups. This process of division of social functions, with the concomitant differentiation of power, cannot be explained by physical gender properties alone. Thus, in many tribal societies it was strictly forbidden for women even to touch weapons or to take part in their manufacture (Harris, 1988: 434–8). Such 'taboos' do not correspond to any inborn abilities or disabilities: they reflect relations of social power which have evolved over time.

The second stage in the long-term process of the monopolisation of physical violence was the formation of a class of professional warriors. The transition to this stage occurred in agrarian societies with an advanced specialisation of functions.

There is some evidence to suggest that 'priests' preceded 'warriors' in forming a profession of their own. It would seem that in several parts of the world—in Mesopotamia, in China, and in Mesoamerica, for instance—the first cities were built around temples containing stores of food and other treasures. In view of the storage function of these temples I think it unlikely that they were ever entirely unguarded. The archæological record appears to suggest, however, that initially they were not strongly fortified.[6]

What the record also shows, and more clearly, is traces of destruction. The first temples were burnt down, and when they were rebuilt, they tended to be walled. The temples evolved into citadels.

Then, at a later stage again, we may observe a demilitarisation of the temples. In some cases this may reflect a genuine demilitarisation of the society of which they formed a part. Far more often, however, the demilitarisation of the temples (or churches) reflected an increasing differentiation of social functions, and a transfer of military power from priests to warriors. Temples became relatively peaceful enclaves in agrarian empires that did not lose their strongly military imprint.

Thus, as early as in the legendary era of Abraham, Palestine was a region that lay within the sphere of influence of military-agrarian empires; the vicissitudes of the people of Israel as described in the books of the Old Testament consist to a large extent of military events—battles, victories, defeats. The Babylonian captivity signified the definitive end of the sovereign military power of an Israelite state, and this military defeat gave new chances of power to the nation's spiritual leaders, the priests.

Greece lay more in the periphery of the great empires of Western Asia, but there too war appears to have been endemic most of the time. A farming life not menaced by war, such as we find depicted by Hesiod, was, in all likelihood, rare. As a true-minded farmer, Hesiod was given to bitter complaints about his terrible plight, but this should not blind us to the fact that his poem bears all the marks of having been written in what must have been an oasis of peace. It is altogether a fascinating source of sociological interpretation, and its author deserves to be regarded as the first ideologue of the Third Estate. Our main theme here is, however, the sociogenesis of the Second Estate, the warrior aristocracy.

Whereas Hesiod hardly refers to military violence at all, it is present in almost every page of Homer's *Iliad* and *Odyssey*. The subject matter of these great poems *is* war. The last sentence of the Book of Judges reads: 'In those days there was no king in Israel; everyone did what was good in his own eyes'. This sentence applies equally well to the world of Odysseus and his peers: they were unruly war-lords, who would sometimes join forces against a common enemy but who would in the last resort always be prepared to take the law into their own hands.

Is Homer then describing the 'war of all against all'? Certainly not in any strict sense. For one thing, in the world of Odysseus military force was already monopolised to a high degree—even if the monopoly was still very far from being as strongly centralised as it was to become many centuries later when the Macedonian kings Philip and Alexander established their hegemony over this area. At Odysseus' time, there was a small upper stratum of highly independent warriors who possessed the material equipment and—no less important—the physical and social-psychological skills, acquired through long and arduous training, which, in combination, were needed to fight a war. The large majority of the population did not take part in the struggles, and could only hope that it would be spared the fate of being raided by an armed band.

Increased productivity, greater numbers, and a higher degree of concentration, specialisation, and organisation all combined to enable people to exploit unprecedented technical possibilities. It was especially the forging of metals, made feasible by enhanced control over fire, which played a crucial role. Having been used at first mostly as ornaments and means of exchange, metals became increasingly important in the manufacture of tools for agriculture and even more so of weapons for warfare (cf. Tylecote, 1987).

The emergence of a warrior class was not simply the function of technological advances in metallurgy, however. The new techniques in armour and weaponry as such were, in turn, conditioned by the increasing specialisation of warriors. In tribal societies the warriors used to be part-time specialists. When there was farming work to do, they would do that (or, if they felt it to be beneath their dignity, they might go hunting). Usually, it was only after the harvest had been reaped that the men went to war. As men, they monopolised warfare, but war continued to be by and large a seasonal activity.

The shift that occurred in more advanced agrarian societies was the rise of full-time warriors—men whose prime occupation in life was not, as in farming, production, but its very opposite: destruction, and who were available for this purpose all year round. Warriors, military men, became professional experts in killing people and burning property, in murder and arson.

Although this may sound like a moral indictment, I do not intend it that way. I merely wish to make a very general factual statement. What specialised full-time warriors in advanced agrarian societies were good at, where their expertise lay, what their particular training, organisation and equipment enabled them to do better than non- specialists was precisely this: large-scale murder and arson. By virtue of their capacity to kill and burn they could overwhelm an agrarian community, capture its property, and—literally—get away with it, the way Odysseus did after his seizure of Ismarus.

The three components—training, organisation and equipment— were, I think, equally important for the emergence of a warrior class. The training consisted not only in learning to handle the equipment of sword and shield, but also in acquiring the habits of command and obedience that were required of the military leader and his troops. Authority in command was necessary to plan the logistics and to coordinate the actual operations of combat as well as to prevent the soldiers from looting for themselves and, in doing so, turning against each other. Odysseus' assurance that after the sack of Ismarus no man went away without his proper share of the booty throws some light on this aspect of military discipline and the way it was sustained by hierarchy.

By themselves, the properties of the warriors as such cannot sufficiently explain their rise as a dominant social class. Several authors, such as the German historian Alexander Rüstow (1950) and the Dutch sociologist Anton Wichers (1965), have pointed out that the process of *Überlagerung* as Rüstow calls it—the 'overcasting' of agrarian society by an upper layer of warriors—can only be explained by the particular *bonding* of warriors and peasants, as protectors and producers. It was in this bonding process that military-agrarian societies took shape.

Although Rüstow himself does not use the concept of 'military-agrarian society', he clearly perceived the power relations underlying this type of society. For an eloquent sketch of the inextricability of these power relations read the following quotation from Wichers:

> The majority of the population had to live scattered and in small units, which considerably impeded popular communication and organisation. Then there was the fact that the harvest and the livestock were so difficult to hide. That harvest, moreover, had previously stood in the field for half a year or longer, vulnerable to destruction. The rural areas lay as it were invitingly open for 'lawful' and unlawful forms of coercion and tribute. Whoever had assembled some cavalry around himself and trained himself to use a sword could subjugate the sedentary population, either gradually from within or suddenly from without. The people, moreover, could not imitate this by equipping and training themselves, for then they would have to neglect their fields. We saw that there were few possibilities for a subsistence outside agriculture, so that the 'saturation limit' of non-agrarians was soon reached. Consequently, there was also only limited room for lords or for cities with lordly ambitions. Once one had such a lordly position, one had one's competitors to fear, but no longer very much the great multitude of the people. The latter would usually rather surrender something than suffer anyone's 'punishments'. Up to the eve of the present century we may observe, therefore, that the frontiers of principalities and other units of rule could change without this making much of an impression upon the majority of the people, let alone their having been consulted. For them all too often it was merely a matter of being bitten by the dog or the cat. (Wichers, 1965: 53)

In making these observations the author is primarily referring to rural Western Europe (and the Northern Netherlands in particular) in the Middle Ages and early modern times. If we replace the cavalry by differently equipped troops, however, his words can serve as a general characteristic of the power structure in the world of Odysseus and in a great many other settings.

The crucial point, for which history provides us with abundant examples, is this: an agrarian community was virtually defenceless against organised military bands—unless it could mobilise an army of its own. This observation, in all its simplicity, can serve to explain what seems to be the functional paradox of warriorhood: *the function of warriors was to fight against other warriors.*[7] The paradox is resolved when we relate it to the basic features of agrarian society. Farmers and peasants lived a life that was (comparatively) productive and vulnerable. Warriors, on the other hand, were unproductive and destructive but ready to fight. Innocuous as it is, this formulation conveys something that is essential to the structure of military-agrarian societies. Given the peasants' productivity and vulnerability and the warriors' powers of destruction and readiness to fight, a combination of the elements of productivity and armed force turned out to be well nigh inevitable for both groups. The warriors needed the peasants for food, the peasants needed the warriors for protection. This unplanned—and, in a profound sense, fatal—combination formed the context for the great variety of mixtures of military protection and economic exploitation that marks the history of the great majority of advanced agrarian societies.

At one extreme was the Odysseus-at-Ismarus variant: a single brief and violent visit to a community that did not enjoy sufficient protection. The opposite pole was formed by the situation that is more familiar to us—of farmers who regularly pay taxes, who may have done some military service when they were young men, and who remain free from visitations by armed troops for the rest of their lives. In between these two poles we may find the finest gradations of looting, extortion, serfdom, and land rent, which form so many variations upon the common theme of the symbiosis of agrarian producers and their military protectors—as analysed comprehensively by writers of different persuasions such as E.L. Jones, John Hall and Michael Mann.[8]

Perhaps it might have been comforting if, at this point, I could say that in actual practice life was not as bad as all that for the peasants, because, after all, they still had their priests. If the warriors threatened to go too far in oppressing and pillaging, the priests would intervene and would, so to speak, chop off the right hand of the warriors. This did not, however, happen very frequently. More often than not, priests and warriors would lend each other a helping hand. As far as I can see, wherever in agrarian societies rural settlements developed into city states which were subsequently engulfed by larger empires, the priests became subservient to the warriors. This shift in the balance of power occurred equally in those cases where the ruling ideology (which usually was a religious ideology) might give a different impression, suggesting that it was the priests who formed the first estate or the highest caste.

I do not think that the great anti-priest, Friedrich Nietzsche, was correct when he proposed that at first there was a regime of warriors that was then taken over by priests through cunning and deceit.[9] If there was a clear succession, it is much more likely to have been the other way around: as societies increasingly came to rely upon crops and livestock, religious-agrarian regimes emerged which later were superseded by military-agrarian regimes. The military elites, understandably, did not always manage to establish working relationships of mutual trust with the majority of the population. This may help to explain their willingness to enter into coalitions with priestly groups who, in their disciplinary role, stood closer to the people and had a firmer grip on them.

5. Further Developments in the Relations between Priests and Warriors

This, then, is how we may envisage the sociogenesis of the three orders. It all began with the intensification of agriculture, which offered special power chances to priests as specialists in orientation and discipline. They helped to subordinate individual to collective interests, and short-term to longer-term interests; this important social function formed the basis of the religious-agrarian regimes which they conducted. However, as the productivity of agrarian communities increased—partly by virtue of the new ecological regime—so did their vulnerability to attack by armed bands. Moreover, in the process of specialisation new crafts emerged, such as smiths, whose mastery over fire enabled them to make weapons of a force and flexibility that enormously increased the destructive powers of the warriors. As a result 'militarisation took command', leaving no single people unaffected. If a group did not wish to be captured by foreign invaders, it had to recruit military specialists out of its own midst who then were in a position to join the ranks of the warrior elite.

Along with the ascendency of warrior groups the religious-agrarian regimes were weakened in another way as well. Agrarian life had long ceased to be a novelty; the need for priestly guidance in sowing and harvesting and in slaughtering animals diminished. Like Hesiod, farmers could handle these tasks themselves.

We can see how, as a result, the element of agrarian discipline gradually receded into the background in the repertory of priestly activities. Thus at the dawn of Christianity, concern with agricultural procedures had virtually disappeared. Christ himself is often said to refer to peasant life, but only for the sake of parables: just as the peasant will separate the wheat from the chaff, so, when the day has come, God will judge men, etc. Rural life had become the familiar context from which similes were chosen, but the problems of farming were not any more the focus upon which the teachings concentrated.

At the time when Christianity originated the agrarian regime was so firmly established in a combination of militarily-backed external supervision and internal self-restraint that regular priestly support was redundant. Moreover, as concentration of the population proceeded, increasing numbers of people came to live in cities. Under these circumstances, the problems ensuing from the conditions of life in a large military empire took precedence over those of agrarian production and storage. It was primarily to the former type of problems that the teachings of Christ were addressed. Christianity and the other great world religions, as Max Weber argued (1922: I, 526–76), are attuned to the ideal of individual salvation—an ideal that seemed particularly appealing to people who found themselves living under the continuous constraints of a society marked by enormously great power differences and, concomitantly, very harsh social relations (as expressed, for example, in the gladiatorial games and in the public executions of prisoners—festive occasions which bear some resemblance to the human sacrifices of the Aztecs[10]). The central redemptory idea of a Kingdom of God—as a Kingdom—may be seen as an idealised reflection of the hierarchical structure of military-agrarian empires.

It remains intriguing that in the societies of the Greeks and Romans, in which for centuries the priestly class had been of little significance, a new priestly organisation, the Christian church, succeeded within a span of less than ten generations in attaining influence over the highest state organs and in making its religion the offical imperial cult. Even more intriguing is the fact that, when a large part of the empire collapsed, this priestly organisation managed to come to terms with the new, 'barbaric', military rulers.

Chapter Six

Short-Term Interests and Long-Term Processes: The Case of Civilisation and Decivilisation

Stephen Mennell[1]

People pursue more or less short-term interests. Their conception of what are those interests is shaped by much longer-term social processes, and so is the time horizon over which they pursue them. And, in turn, their actions in pursuit of more or less short-term interests interweave, in a way that involves many unforeseen and unintended consequences, to produce long-term processes which are largely blind and unplanned but nevertheless have discernible structure.

Economic theory, together with its more recent outgrowth known as 'rational choice' theory in political science and sociology, deals elegantly and parsimoniously with the pursuit of more or less short-term interests. It has not hitherto greatly concerned itself with very long-term processes. As his contributions to this volume show, however, Eric Jones—whose intellectual orientation stems from economic theory—has urged on economic historians the necessity of taking much longer time perspectives.

Historical sociology, on the other hand, has concerned itself with how people's conception of their interests is shaped within processes of social development, often representing it in a highly deterministic way. A major intellectual challenge is to be found in integrating rational choice theory and historical sociology to advance our understanding of long-term processes. Abram de Swaan, in his study (1988) of the development of collective provision in five countries since the Middle

Ages, has made an ambitious start on this task. Besides rational choice theory he has employed particularly the work of Norbert Elias, which is also the major influence on Johan Goudsblom. The present chapter takes this as its cue to present a preliminary exploration of how short-term interests and long-term processes may be related in the cases of civilising and decivilising processes. The first section briefly presents the theory of civilising processes; the second introduces some of the much less historically grounded and more 'timeless' ideas of 'rational choice theory'; and the third section takes up the question of 'decivilising' episodes in history, and in particular the problem of why they often seem to proceed with greater speed than their civilising counterparts.

1. Civilising and Decivilising Processes

I shall not use the term 'civilisation' with all its popular meanings, nor in the very general sense of large-scale complex society or culture area employed by writers like Spengler and Toynbee. When I use the term 'civilising process', I am using it in the specific technical sense developed by Norbert Elias. My particular interest is in *decivilising* processes. Decivilising processes are what happens when civilising processes go into reverse. I shall therefore have to say a good deal about Elias's theory of civilising processes in order to explain what kinds of evidence I am seeking in an investigation of decivilising processes.[2]

Elias speaks of civilising processes on two levels.[3] The first is the *individual level*, and is rather uncontroversial. Infants and children have to acquire through learning the adult standards of behaviour and feeling prevalent in their society; to speak of this as a civilising process is just to use another term for 'socialisation'. That this process has a typical structure and sequence is not disputed. But the second level is more controversial. Where did these standards come from? They have not always existed, nor always been the same. Elias argues it is possible to identify long-term civilising processes in the shaping of standards of behaviour and feeling over many generations within particular cultures. Again, the idea that these standards change is not controversial; what generates controversy is that the changes take the form of *structured processes* of change with a discernible—though largely unplanned— *direction* over time. This problem of direction is crucial, for my interest is in reversals in civilising processes on these two levels, and the notion of reversal makes sense only if one is confident that the process was previously moving in a structured way in a recognisable direction. Many of the symptoms of civilising and decivilising processes are not so easily measured as—though they are not unconnected with—trends in economic production or in population.

Despite his very extensive publications in the 1970s and 1980s, Elias is still best known for the two volumes of *The Civilising Process*, first published obscurely in 1939 but not available in English until more than forty years later, and they remain the central point of reference for his work. The first volume is the better known, dealing with the history of manners in Western Europe from the late Middle Ages to the Victorian period. The second is a detailed study of the process of state formation, again in Europe, since the Dark Ages.

The basic idea, and the basic link between the two halves, is that there is a connection between the long-term structural development of societies and long-term changes in people's social character or typical personality make-up. In other words, as the structure of societies becomes more complex, manners, culture and personality also change in a particular and discernible direction, first among élite groups, then gradually more widely. This is worked out with great subtlety for Western Europe since the Middle Ages. But it is a weakness that *The Civilising Process* is based entirely on European evidence. It is not so much that it is Euro*centric* as that it is *about* Europe, and specifically about the process of development through which Europeans—by the time they began to use 'civilisation' as a badge of what they supposed to be their superiority over other, non-European peoples—had almost entirely forgotten their own ancestors had passed. But inevitably it is not always perfectly clear which aspects of Elias's theory apply to Europe alone, and which are of more general validity.

Doubts about how generalisable are various aspects of the theory centre especially on Elias's theory of state formation. Implicitly Elias begins from Max Weber's definition of the state as an organisation which successfully upholds a claim to binding rule-making over a territory, by virtue of commanding a monopoly of the legitimate use of violence (Weber, 1922: I, 54), but he is more interested in the *process* through which a monopoly of the means of violence (*and* taxation) is established and extended. After the Dark Ages in which centrifugal forces were dominant, leading to political and economic fragmentation and feudalisation, centripetal forces regained dominance in a process of state-formation. A particularly vivid feature of his theory of state-formation is his model of the 'elimination contest' between numerous rival territorial magnates, a process with a compelling sequential dynamic through which successively larger territorial units emerge with more effective central monopoly apparatuses.

It is well known that the pattern of relatively small and relatively effective states which emerged in Europe differs in quite significant ways from that of the regimes elsewhere which in their various aspects are referred to as agrarian empires, oriental despotisms and revenue pumps. Elias's account of the state-formation process in Europe emphasises the initially relatively small disparities between many small territories, and subsequently the fluctuating though gradually more relatively even balances between contending elements within the emerging states (cf. Jones, 1981; Hall, 1985). These conditions were probably not widely met elsewhere. I want to argue, however, that even if Elias's model of state formation fits the European case best and is not perfectly generalisable elsewhere, that does not invalidate his more general theory of civilising processes. Nor for my own purposes does it invalidate the comparative investigation of decivilising processes. There are two reasons for that. First it could be argued that *how* the monopolisation of violence comes about is less important to Elias's argument than the fact of its being achieved. That is because one of Elias's central arguments is that

> if in a particular region, the power of central authority grows, if over a larger or smaller area people are *forced* to live at peace with one another, the moulding of the affects and the standards of the demands made upon emotional management are very gradually changed as well. (1939: I, 201, my italics; translation modified to reflect Elias's later terminology)

The second reason is that Elias does not put *all* his eggs in the state formation basket. State formation, he argues, is only one process interweaving with others to enmesh individuals in increasingly complex \webs of interdependence. It interweaves with the division of labour, the growth of trade, towns, the use of money and administrative apparatuses, and increasing population in a spiral process. Internal pacification of territory facilitates trade, which facilitates the growth of towns and division of labour and generates taxes which support larger administrative and military organisations, which in turn facilitate the internal pacification of larger territories, and so on—a cumulative process experienced as a compelling force by people caught up in it. Furthermore, according to Elias, the gradually higher standards of habitual self-restraint engendered in people contribute in turn to the upward spiral—being necessary for example to the formation of gradually more effective and calculable administration. Equally, the loss of certain *learned* 'psychological' capacities could contribute to a downward spiral. But it is not so much a matter of identifying single causal factors as of tracing how various causal strands interweave over time to produce an overall process with increasing momentum. In the same way, when turning to decivilising processes, and looking at a case like the Roman Empire, it is less necessary to point to a single factor—barbarian invasions, christianity, lead pipes or whatever—than to build a 'process theory' (Mennell, 1989a: 177ff) showing how various strands interweave to reinforce a downward spiral.

It should be borne in mind here that, in contrast with Western Europe, ancient empires or oriental despotisms have often been depicted as monopoly apparatuses floating like a raft on a largely unchanging, largely autarkic agrarian economy. In that case the interweaving with the division of labour, etc., would be much weaker, and most likely weaker in its psychological effects. That could well make a downward spiral easier to set in motion.

What about the manners side of the argument? If violence is so central to Elias's underlying problematic, why does his book begin by looking at all those instances of disgusting medieval manners for which he is most famous—the development of conventions about eating, washing, spitting, blowing one's nose, urinating and defecating, undressing? He focused particularly on these most basic, 'natural' or 'animalic' of human functions because these are things human beings cannot bio-logically avoid doing, no matter what society, culture or age they live in. Moreover, infants are born in the same emotional condition everywhere, so that the *lifetime* point of departure is always the same. Therefore if change occurs in the way these functions are handled, it can be seen rather clearly. But his underlying concern is with topics more central to the interests of social theorists then and now: violence and aggressiveness. In Europe at least, these became more tamed and more hidden behind the scenes of social life along with defecation, nakedness and the rest.

Elias puts forward an elaborate theory of changing personality formation. He argues that as webs of interdependence become denser and more extensive, there gradually takes place a shift in the balance between external constraints (*Fremdzwänge*—constraints by others) and self-constraints, in favour of the latter. His book on time and timing (1984) brings out particularly clearly the link between social and personality changes arising from the necessity of coordinating more and more complicated sequences of activities. The pressures on individuals to exercise greater *foresight* take various forms: Elias discusses particularly the processes of rationalisation, 'psychologisation', and the advance of thresholds of shame and embarrassment.[4]

Psychologisation is linked to the idea that spreading webs of interdependence tend to be associated with *relatively* more equal power ratios and 'functional democratisation', meaning more and more reciprocal controls between more and more social groups. Less abstractly: 'more people are forced more often to pay more attention to more other people' (Goudsblom, 1989: 722). This produces pressures towards greater consideration of the consequences of one's own actions for other people on whom one is more or less dependent, and there tends in consequence to be an increase in 'mutual identification'. This idea is not new to Elias—it was expressed very clearly by Alexis de Tocqueville[5]—but it has a very direct bearing on matters of violence and cruelty. *The advance of thresholds of shame and embarrassment* also involves increased foresight, in the sense of greater vigilance in anticipating social dangers, especially the transgression of various social prohibitions.

Rationalisation, warns Elias, has no absolute beginning in human history. Just as there is no point at which human beings suddenly began to possess a 'conscience', there is none before which they were completely 'irrational'. Still more misleading is it to think of rationality as some kind of property of individual minds in isolation from each other. 'There is not actually a "ratio", there is at most "rationalisation"' (1939: II, 277). What actually changes is the way people are bonded with each other in society and, in consequence, the moulding of personality structure. Elias's argument is that the forms of behaviour we call 'rationality' are produced within a social figuration in which an extensive transformation of external compulsions into internal compulsions takes place:

> The complementary concepts of 'rationality' and 'irrationality' refer to the relative parts played by short-term affects and long-term conceptual models of observable reality in individual behaviour. The greater the importance of the latter in the delicate balance between affective and reality-orientated commands, the more 'rational' is behaviour . . . (1969: 92)

Although he avoids the words, Elias clearly has in mind Freud's 'Pleasure Principle' and 'Reality Principle'. What is involved in any process of rationalisation is a central component of the civilising process, the increasingly sharp differentiation of the outward-directed, reality-orientated psychological functions. A more 'rationally' functioning consciousness is less directly coloured by drive impulses and affective fantasies (1939: II, 286), and is more inclined to defer the gratification of short-term affects in order to achieve longer-term goals by means given (via conceptual apparatuses) by the external reality of social interdependences.

It follows that the type of reality-orientated conceptual model involved in the control of human behaviour varies with the structure of social reality itself. That is why the 'court-rationality' of courtiers was different from the 'economic rationality' of the commercial and professional bourgeoisie (Elias, 1969: 92–3). In the one, it is people and prestige that are made calculable as instruments of power; in the other, it is economic opportunities, financial gains and losses. Each could appear irrational from the point of view of the other. The courtier's rank dictated expenditure heedless of income, and appeared mere extravagance to the merchant; yet, conversely, for a courtier to economise like a bourgeois could involve a serious loss of the prestige and rank that was the principal goal in a social stratum so constituted. Yet both these forms of rationality have in common the preponderance of longer-term reality-orientated considerations over short-term affects in the control of behaviour in particular social fields.

There is not space here to discuss Elias's complex theory of the development of modes of knowledge and their relations to civilising processes and other cultural trends (see Elias, 1987; Mennell, 1989a: 159–99), but mention needs to be made of one aspect of it relevant to decivilising processes. In a sophisticated reworking of ideas, some of which can be traced back as far as Comte and the Victorian anthropologist Edward Tylor, Elias makes a connection between, on the one hand, the prevailing level of danger (and, conversely, the level of control which people have over the forces which affect their lives) and, on the other hand, the relative degree of detachment (and, conversely, the degree of emotional involvement and fantasy-loading) in their modes of knowledge. He stresses the interdependence between trends in any society in (a) control over extra-human forces ('nature'), (b) control over interpersonal or social forces, and (c) people's control over themselves as individuals ('psychological' controls).[6] Although in *very* long-term perspective all three may have tended to grow, he emphasises how difficult initial advances are, given that for example advances in control over natural dangers may bring with them changes in social relations (e.g. longer chains of interdependence) which then become *more* difficult to control, increasing the danger which people pose *for each other*, and making it more difficult to achieve more detached and less fantasy-laden forms of knowledge.

It can now be seen that the growth of pressures towards greater foresight in many forms is a central element in the theory of civilising processes.[7] Because the vocabulary in which it is expressed, and the *problématique* in which it is embedded, are very different from those of economics, it is easy to overlook an important point: what is described in the context of historical sociology as the growth of pressures towards greater *foresight* can be expressed in the vocabulary of economics and rational choice theory as changes in the *time horizon* for decision-making, or as changes in the *rate of time preference*. Note, however, that we are talking of long*er*, not long, time horizons over which people pursue their interests; individual people's perceptions of their interests are not long in comparison with the long-term social processes that are our concern in this volume, for, as Keynes famously remarked, in the long run we are all dead.

2. Rational Choice: Alternative Explanation or Supplementary Model?

'Rational choice theory' is an unfortunate appelation, for the name seems to imply that there exists an eternal, perhaps innate, unchanging human quality of rationality. That would seem to put it at odds with

Elias's theory of civilising processes, as well as with the Weberian tradition in sociology, which have been concerned with the changing patterning of human rationality in the course of social development. But this contradiction is more apparent than real. One of the basic methodological assumptions of rational choice theory is that only via the concept of rationality can the actions of others become intelligible *as* action. If we are to offer 'intentional' explanations of actions—or, in other words, if we are to say that we 'understand' the actions of others—we can only do so by interpreting it as in some sense rational. But in what sense? Only in the minimal sense that *all* (normal) human beings have the capacity to choose ends and pursue them by means available to them. In this sense, as Elias always insists, there is no zero-point in human rationality. In his discussion of rational*isation*, he is concerned with the changing patterns and elaboration of this universal human capcity, especially as it is patterned in larger and increasingly more complicated societies. As we have noted, rationalisation is to be seen as involving a change in the *balance* between affective and reality-orientated impulses, and an associated lengthening of the time horizons over which means-ends chains are pursued. Moreover Elias demonstrated that the behaviour of courtiers, which could easily be seen as 'irrational', actually involved a strong rationalisation spurt of its own kind.

Rational choice theory is for the most part thoroughly ahistorical. It does not seem to me to offer an *alternative* explanation for the processes of development with which Elias is concerned—nor indeed has it much to say directly about any of the very long-term processes with which this volume is concerned. Nevertheless, rational choice theory has some value and interest as a supplementary model which helps to clarify certain aspects of the theory of civilising processes.

The 'structural' side of Elias's discussion of the European civilising process is much concerned with the growth of collective arrangements—states and related institutions like armies, courts, administrations, fiscal apparatuses, along with the growth of towns and trade and the use of money—many of which, in the terminology of economics and rational choice theory, are or involve 'collective goods'. These social arrangements, in Elias's account, arise not out of anyone's long-term strategy, but out of the largely unplanned consequences of the interweaving actions of individuals and small groups pursuing their own interests

within longer and longer chains of interdependence. Again translating
into the alternative terminology, these proceses are rich in externalities
and in associated 'free rider' problems. Eric Jones is quite right to claim
that 'unintended consequences have always been the concern of the
economist' (page 59 above)—economists usually speak of the 'unintended aggregate effects' of many individual decisions (the idea is also
similar to Goudsblom's 'Reception Effect')—and the problem of collective action is also central to rational choice theory.

In economics, it was Kenneth Arrow (1951; cf. Coleman, 1986: 63–84)
who particularly posed the problem of collective action in his famous
'impossibility theorem'—concerning the apparent impossibility of constructing a collective utility function from the conflicting rank order of
preferences of individual actors. Traditional sociological theories can
be classified according to the means by which they implicitly solve
Arrow's impossibility theorem. 'Conflict' theories dwell on the power
of certain social groups to impose—after struggles—their preferences
over those of other groups. 'Consensus' theories tend to look at
ways—usually non-conflictful, with a strong emphasis on socialisation
or enculturation—in which common agreement emerges on a shared
scale of preferences. (Theories using the Gramscian notion of 'hegemony', and similar ideas of 'manipulated consensus' or 'dominant
ideology', take on aspects of both these approaches.) And the 'exchange'
tradition pays attention to how the reciprocal exchange of benefits leads
through contractual relations to the common advantage.[8] Both rational
choice theory and Elias's theory are subversive of all these traditional
approaches in their pure forms,[9] though they can and do take on certain
elements of all three.

Elias's theory, it is important to note, does *not* rest on the assumption
that large groups of individuals with common interests will usually
attempt to further those common interests. In that, it differs both from
sociological theories of the value-consensus kind and from the many
varieties of Marxism which share this assumption in different ways.
This gives Elias's theory a point of contact with rational choice theory,
one of the major contributions to which—Mancur Olson's *The Logic
of Collective Action* (1965)—set out systematically to refute just that
assumption.

Olson sought to demonstrate[10] that even if each of the individuals in
a large group were rational and self-interested, and even if each of them

would individually gain if they achieved their common group interest, it does *not* follow that they would act to achieve their objective. He argues that:

> If the members of a large group rationally seek to maximise their personal welfare, this will *not* act to advance their common or group objectives unless there is coercion to force them to do so, or unless some separate incentive, separate from the achievement of the common or group interest, is offered to the members of the group individually on the condition that they help to bear the costs or burdens involved in the achievement of the group objectives. (1965: 2)[11]

That Elias had already in the 1930s taken this point on board is most evident in his discussion of the 'elimination contest' between rival territorial magnates in Europe around the beginning of the second millennium AD.[12] The internal pacification of larger and larger territories is, as he makes clear (see page 96 above), a public good which can only be imposed by force, not by altruistic agreement on peaceful values. Only in response, under the impact of forcefully imposed relative peace, does 'the moulding of affects' change as well. Conversely, the constant violent conflicts over land in the course of the elimination contest were in no way simply the 'result' of people's aggressive motivation. On the contrary, the competitive pressure was generated by the particular way in which warrior lords were socially inter-dependent with each other—by the structure of the game in which they were involved. The magnate *had* to fight with neighbours to extend his territory. In some abstract philosophical sense a magnate with, for the period, an unusually pacific temperament was 'free' to choose merely to try to hold on to his existing domains and avoid conflict with his neighbours. But the consequences of such a course of action were perfectly plain: anyone who declined to compete, merely conserving his property while others strove to increase theirs, necessarily ended up smaller and weaker than the others, and was in ever-increasing danger of succumbing to them (1939: II, 43). Each knew that if his neighbour acquired more land—even if from a third party rather than from himself—the increased economic and military resources it brought meant inevitably that the balance of power between him and his neighbour was tilted to his own disadvantage, and it was extremely probable that sooner or later his domains would be invaded, his army defeated, his lands absorbed by the more powerful neighbour, and he and his family killed. As to the overall objective, control of land, there was little scope for choice; as to the means of attaining it, there were a few alternative tactics—strategic marriages were sometimes an alternative to fighting, for example—but in games theoretic parlance, the feasible set was limited.

Both rational choice theory and Elias avoid the 'oversocialised conception of man' (Wrong, 1961) into which many varieties of sociology have fallen.[13] In Elias's conception, norms and values are scarcely ever absorbed into the personality during the individual 'civilising process' without problems; there are always costs and benefits to conformity as well as to the breaking of social norms and conventions (1939: II, 243). In rational choice theory, too, though its psychological assumptions are primitive in comparison with Elias's, norms and values are never seen as absolute wall-like barriers even in the most traditionally organised societies:

> [T]here are innumerable examples of traditional behaviour being discarded when new opportunities become available—not because they are better embodiments of the value inherent in customary behaviour, but because the individual finds they serve his goal better. (Elster, 1986: 23)

More important, both approaches seek to *explain* social norms, rather than taking them as givens in the determination of people's conduct.[14] In the case of Elias's long-term historical investigations, that aim scarcely requires further comment. In the case of rational choice theory, an example of how a norm might be explained is the case of the mafia convention of *omertà*—silence—which can be seen as a means of overcoming the Prisoners' Dilemma and obtaining the optimal outcome.

There is indeed a huge literature on the Prisoners' Dilemma type of game (see for example Ullmann-Margalit, 1978, and Schotter, 1981), and it is central to rational choice theory. It is easy to see why. It poses in archetypical form the problem of how social co-operation is possible between interdependent people where each has the potential both to aid and to harm the other and where each is uncertain of the other's probable response to the situation. In summary:

> Two guilty prisoners, against whom there is not enough incriminating evidence, are interrogated separately. Each faces two alternative ways of

acting: to confess the crime or to keep silent. They both know that if neither confesses, they will be convicted of some minor offence, concerning which there is sufficient evidence against them, and will be sentenced to a year in prison. If both confess, each will be sentenced to five years in prison. However, if only one confesses, he thereby turns king's evidence and is thus set free, whereas the other receives a heavy term of ten years. (Ullmann-Margalit, 1978: 18)

How is co-operation achieved in the face of this type of dilemma? Several answers have been advanced within the rational choice tradition. Rapoport, in an early contribution, argued that individual rationality alone was an inadequate starting point for rational choice theory, and that social values must be brought into consideration *ab initio*. In his discussion of the Prisoners' Dilemma, he pointed out that the outcome generally considered the most likely, where both prisoners confess—minimising the maximum loss (thus reaching the 'minimax' or 'maximin' position)—actually depends on making some inferences about how other people will behave. Different assumptions would lead to a different outcome:

Instead of taking as the basis of calculations the question 'Where am I better off?', suppose each prisoner starts with the following basic assumption: 'My partner is like me. Therefore he is likely to act like me. If I conclude that I should confess, he will probably conclude the same. If I conclude that I should not confess, this is the way he probably thinks. In the first case, we both get -5; in the second case, we both get +5. This indicates that I personally benefit by not confessing.' (Rapoport, 1960: 175)

This assumption of *similarity* is theoretically interesting. It may be particularly plausible in a case like the Prisoner's Dilemma, where the two prisoners are personally known to each other, but it also seems to operate in a wider context. For instance, it has the effect of solving the difficulty which rational choice theory encounters when trying to explain voting behaviour:

The assumption of similarity is indeed the rationale which induces the individual citizen to vote. The argument that a single vote 'makes no appreciable difference' is countered with 'Yes, but if everyone thought so, the will of the collective would find no expression'. This is the rationale behind any co-operative effort. (Rapoport, 1960: 177)

I would like tentatively to suggest that Elias's discussion of the conditions for the growth of a wider sense of mutual identification is relevant here, for that deals precisely with the growth of the sense that other people, *whom one does not necessarily know personally*, are probably rather similar to oneself, with similar feelings and likely to behave in a similar way. Note that this is subtly very different from the assumption that consensus on specific common values or the identification of common group interests will lead automatically to group action in pursuit of those values or interests.

Nevertheless, Rapoport's similiarity assumption was much criticised. He commented that

> our habits of thought (including definitions of rationality, etc.) are too deeply ingrained in terms of individuals and their individual interests abstracted from a more inclusive context. We have difficulty in making social values the fundamental starting point of our definition of rationality. . . . [W]e have been too long accustomed to the uncritical acceptance of the laissez-faire principle, namely, that a totality of individuals seeking their respective self-interests by *shortsighted* calculations actually will move towards the realisation of this self-interest by the operation of economic laws derived from the assumptions of a free competitive market economy. (1960: 176, 177)

In more recent years, several other solutions to the problem of co-operation have been advanced which purport to make Rapoport's similiarity assumption unnecessary. Most of these depend on relaxing one or other of the assumptions of the basic Prisoners' Dilemma. Axelrod's (1984) theory of co-operation, however, does not. It rests instead on recognising that the most misleading thing about the model is that it consists of a single isolated episode. More frequently, in real life, people face whole sequences of such situations, and they know that they are likely to meet and confront fellow players in the future. So, in Axelrod's game theoretic account of the evolution of co-operation, foresight is certainly helpful (1984: 22).[15]

That brings us back once more to Elias's discussion of the pattern of social development necessary for, and conducive to, people acquiring the capacity to exercise *foresight*, and thus to make their calculations over a longer time horizon. This, as we have noted, involves a changing balance between external and internal constraints in the control of behaviour. And this in turn draws attention to the socialisation process (the individual 'civilising process') through which these characteristics are inculcated, and to how changes in that process come about in the context of overall social development (social civilising—or decivilising —processes). Here there is a passing difficulty in reconciling the perspective of the long-term historical sociologist with that of the rational choice theorist. For it must be remembered that when Elias speaks of the growth of foresight, he always emphasises that though long-term processes are generated by many interdependent people pursuing their interests with varying degrees of foresight, such processes overall are unplanned, unintended and 'blind'.

One way of resolving the difficulty—compatible, I think, with both approaches—is to introduce a selection mechanism into models of social development, on the analogy (more or less) of natural selection in Darwinian theory. This is what Axelrod did: his is an *evolutionary* rational choice theory of co-operative behaviour, working through trial and error. An element of this is already implicit in parts of Elias's work (though he is careful to deny that he is a 'social evolutionist' in the general sense). For example, a cautious, pacific, unaggressive modern person would not be best suited to prosper in the medieval elimination contest. Chains of interdependence were short. The threats to existence were those of violence from outside, ever-present but unpredictable. It was neither necessary nor possible for a warrior knight to anticipate the effects of his or anyone else's actions many moves ahead down several links in the chain. Foresight was never one of the greatest knightly virtues: nothing compelled it. On the contrary, impetuosity, swift wrath and uninhibited violence, the savage joys of battle with for the moment no thought ahead, no fear of death or of the torture and mutilation which could follow defeat—all these were positive advantages in a society so organised (1939: II, 236–7, 240). On the other hand, these qualities sometimes persisted long after they had ceased to be advantageous. Elias is fond of citing the Duc de Montmorency, who rebelled against the French king in 1632 (1939: II, 279; 1969: 195). Finding himself confronting the royal army in what should have been a strong position for him, his furious impulse to give battle could not be restrained even long enough to move his guns and troops into position. He galloped forward with a few followers, who were easily cut down; he was put on trial and beheaded soon afterwards. At this stage, foresight and self-control even in battle had become far more indispensable than in medieval times.

Selection mechanisms of this kind have a particular appeal to social scientists who are sceptical of the image of *homo economicus*, of human beings as individuals constantly making careful calculations as to the best strategy for maximising their own utility. An awareness of the largely unplanned quality of social development fuels this scepticism. The standard reply by economists and rational choice theorists is that rational choice models may be psychologically unrealistic, but if they succeed in predicting important aspects of behaviour—as it is claimed they do—that is all that matters: to predict is to explain. But rational choice theory is not omnipotent, and the notion of maximisation—especially in situations of uncertainty—often seems impossibly vague as well as psychologically unrealistic. One solution which has occasionally appealed to economists, such as Alchian (1950) and Nelson and Winter (1982) is to treat economic decisions as solutions hit upon at least partly at random, the most successful among which are then 'selected' and the least successful eliminated by market forces.

This argument fits particularly well with the theory of 'satisficing' behaviour, which Herbert Simon (1957; see also March, 1978) advanced as a psychologically more realistic alternative to the maximising model. According to this theory, people do not seek the best alternative in the feasible set, but limit themselves to what seems to be 'good enough' or satisfactory. They do not engage in constant calculations to maximise profits, to find the latest and best technology, or adopt the most efficient mode of internal organisation. They proceed rather by rule of thumb, and are precipitated into new rules only when the old ones no longer work reasonably well—when evolutionary selection threatens, so to speak.[16]

The theory of satisficing behaviour, along with the recognition that though there are social analogies to evolutionary selection mechanisms they do not operate with constant ruthlessness at all times and places, has considerable appeal to the sociologist and student of long-term social processes. It squares very well, for example, with the 'survival of the mediocre' to which Hallpike (1986: 81–145) has drawn attention.

Where does this leave the notion of maximisation? First, as Eric Jones remarks (page 53 above), 'Not everyone need be engaged in maximising on every margin at once'. Yet to be no more precise than to say that people 'satisfice' would probably leave us with insufficient grounds for Jones's assumption of a growth propensity widespread in human society. Jones suggests that:

> All that is needed is to accept that a desire to reduce material poverty is commonplace in our species, as well it might be considering that poverty exacts such a penalty in terms of dead babies, or at any rate of babies without shoes. A certain inquisitiveness about how things work—things, that is, including markets—and a modicum of human creativity are ancillary postulates. (Jones, p. 53 above)

In the more formal terms of rational choice theory, this boils down simply to the proposition (already mentioned above) that if new elements are added to the choice set, behaviour will change if one of them is seen as better than the formerly top-ranked alternative. The change need not occur immediately. Change involves adjustment costs, and before incurring them rational actors will wait until they are sure the change is a durable one.

This minimal assumption, I suggest, is sufficient not only to give Jones his 'propensity for [extensive] growth . . . widely present in human society', but—through unintended aggregate effects working like compound interest—to produce the long-term dominant trend towards the division of labour. And that in turn has been the fundamental driving force for many other long-term social processes, including civilising processes. But, *pace* Anne Mayhew, this minimal assumption is not an Elemental Human Strategy which 'must empty the interest from the workings of the economy and distract attention from the institutions which are the proper object of study' (Jones, pp. 53–4 above). On the contrary, the institutions are precisely what define in all their variety the structures of the games and the choice sets in which people exhibit this general propensity. But there are no short cuts: the institutions and structures still have to be studied.

What, then, are the deficiencies of economic-cum-rational-choice theory as applied to the study of long-term processes? Its weakness is not, as is often argued (for example by Hindess, 1988), that it reduces social processes to individual choices. If that were so, we should not have have been able to find as many points of compatibility as we have with a writer like Elias who has long campaigned against the *homo clausus* image of the isolated individual. Its principal weakness, as De Swaan (1988) argues, lies rather in its static assumptions.

This is seen most clearly in its handling of the problem of collective action, externalities, and public goods. Discussion of collective action in the rational choice tradition, says De Swaan, takes for granted the pre-existence *of the collectivity* in question.[17] By reformulating the problem in terms of the *sociogenesis of collectivities*, De Swaan seeks to show that the dilemmas of collective action are more apparent than real—or, more exactly, they are the product of rational choice theorists' static assumptions. Thus, since Adam Smith at least, defence has been recognised as a common good, but common in relation to the taken-for-granted collectivity of the nation-state. It is the sociogenesis of collectivities—associations, municipalities, states, and now associations of states—that provides a missing theoretical link:

> In the sociogenetic view, the dilemmas of collective action are a transitory phenomenon: one which belongs to an intermediate stage, when agents are already interdependent and aware of this interdependence without their actions being coordinated yet at a higher level of integration, that of the collectivity. In the course of the collectivising process, collective action produces both a collectivity capable of coordinating the actions of its members effectively and a collective good which corresponds to this level of integration, but can not exist apart from it. (De Swaan, 1988: 4)

De Swaan's book is a pioneering attempt to use both rational choice theory and Eliasian sociology to answer the question of 'How and why did people come to develop collective and compulsory arrangements to cope with deficiencies and adversities that appeared to affect them separately and to call for individual remedies?' (De Swaan, 1988: 2). Here externalities are involved in the shape of 'the indirect consequences of one person's deficiency or adversity for others not immediately afflicted themselves'.

The interdependence between the rich and the poor, the strong and the weak, has always been rich in externalities. In feudal times it could be seen rather clearly that the poor represented both a danger and an opportunity to more powerful groups. They (especially, but not solely, beggars and bandits) posed a threat of physical attack upon persons and property. Simultaneously they constituted a resource for use as workers and as soldiers in power struggles among competing elites.

Later too, the poor were seen as both a threat to public order and public health and as a reserve of potential workers, recruits, consumers and political supporters.

But these external costs and benefits of poverty affected the elites collectively. Separately, no single powerful person or faction could ward off the threat from the poor, nor exploit the potential benefits. That could only be achieved collectively, and here the familiar problem of the 'free rider' arises: 'any joint effort on the part of the rich to control the "externalities" or to exploit the opportunities the poor offered, might also benefit those among the established ranks who had not contributed to it'. To the established groups in society, the problem of poverty thus represents a problem of collective action, and a major thesis of De Swaan's is that 'The dynamics of the collectivising process in poor relief, health care and education stem largely from the conflicts among the elites over the creation of collective goods and the distribution of costs among them.' (1988: 3)

One example of this is the problem of mass epidemics, notably cholera, in the nineteenth century. They were seen to be the consequences of living conditions among the urban poor, but germs knew no social boundaries. By the middle of the century, the technical means of meeting the problem—mains water and sewers—were recognised, but they required immense effort and considerable tax increases, straining the capacity of administrative apparatuses and citizens' willingness to pay. Those who had moved out to new, healthier, and respectable neighbourhoods were often supplied with mains water and sanitation by private subscription, and they often opposed public expenditure on providing these services for the urban slums. Only when the slums were connected to the mains compulsorily and at public expense did water and sewerage networks become a truly public good.

The 'collectivising process' as studied by De Swaan is one aspect of the European civilising process. But his use of rational choice theory has wider implications for the study of social development and economic growth. For example, Goudsblom's accounts in this volume of the rise of priests and warriors in agrarian societies may be seen in these more abstract terms as instances of how human groups overcome free-rider problems and achieve co-operative arrangements in the face of situations resembling the Prisoners' Dilemma.[18] And similarly, the *extensive* growth discussed by Jones, as well as intensive, implies investment (and therefore saving, restraint) in co-operative effort acting as an integrating force.

All the same, though these abstract models may prove of some use in examining and intepreting and connecting together the empirical record of long-term development, they do not subsitute for it. In the next section, I shall return a little closer to the historical record in trying to show in a preliminary way how a similar combination of rational choice theory and Eliasian sociology may be helpful in studying the interweaving of short-term interests and long-term processes within decivilising episodes, and in particular in accounting for the relative rapidity of decivilising processes in comparison with the slow uphill grind of civilising processes.

3. Decivilising Processes: Short-Term and Long-Term

Overall, Elias's work has often been understood as a kind of Victorian progress theory. It is not. He often stresses that civilising processes are reversible. He also stresses that there are many counter-spurts within the process, so that the main trend is visible only in the long view. For example, in the late Middle Ages, while part of the old warrior class in Western Europe was being tamed and transformed into courtiers, other elements of the same class who were not caught up in courts actually became *more* violent and aggressive in their lifestyle under the pressure of the erosion of their social base (Maso, 1982; Mennell, 1989a: 80). As Goudsblom observes, 'It may not be a bad rule of thumb, and not an unsound research strategy to assume that for any given trend a counter-trend may be found, operating in the opposite direction' (page 22 above). The accompanying table summarises the main features of civilising trends and possible symptoms of decivilising counter-trends.

What Elias does assert is that, in the *very* long term, integration processes have predominated over disintegration processes. The 'survival units' in which humans live—inside which levels of violence are relatively low compared with violence between survival units—have become larger. Taagepera (1978) has demonstrated quantitatively how, after the collapse of each of the great empires in the Old World, the next succeeeding one managed to integrate a larger geographical area than its precursor. And for all their prejudices against 'progress theories', few sociologists or anthropologists doubt that on the whole

EUROPEAN CIVILISING PROCESS

STRUCTURAL PROCESSES

⇑ State-formation:
  Monopolisation of means of violence and taxation
⇑ Division of Labour/Social Functions/Heterogeneity
⇑ Trade, towns, money, markets, population

All interweaving to produce longer chains, denser webs of interdependence, with consequences:

⇑ Multipolar control
⇑ More even power ratios
⇑ Functional democratisation

CHANGES IN MANNERS/CULTURE

⇑ Movement "behind the scenes" (bodily functions etc., *and violence*)
⇑ Diminishing contrasts, increasing varieties
⇑ Mutual identification (inc. ⇓ cruelty to humans, animals)

CHANGES IN SOCIAL HABITUS

⇑ Pressures towards foresight:
  - Psychologisation
  - Rationalisation
  - Advancing thresholds of shame and embarrassment
⇑ distance between child's and adult standards

No zero-point in self-constraint, but becomes
  ⇑ more automatic
  ⇑ more even and continuous
  ⇑ more all-round, all-embracing

Taming of aggressiveness

CHANGES IN MODES OF KNOWLEDGE

⇑ Detachment, ⇓ Involvement
  ⇓ fantasy content, ⇑ "reality-congruence"

POSSIBLE SYMPTOMS OF DECIVILISING PROCESSES

STRUCTURAL PROCESSES

Breaking links, shorter chains of Interdependence

⇑ Homogeneity, cellular structure

⇑ danger level, incalculability

CHANGES IN MANNERS/CULTURE

⇑ Re-emergence of violence, etc., into public sphere

⇓ mutual identification, ⇑ cruelty

CHANGES IN SOCIAL HABITUS

⇓ Pressures restraining expression of impulses

⇓ gap child/adult standards

⇑ reliance on external constraints
  ⇑ impulsive
  ⇓ uniformity
  ⇑ exceptions

Freer expression of aggressiveness

CHANGES IN MODES OF KNOWLEDGE

⇑ Involvement, ⇓ Detachment
  ⇑ fantasy content, ⇓ "reality congruence"

more complex societies have arisen out of less complex. So Elias is probably right to pay more attention to civilising than decivilising trends.

Decivilising processes presuppose civilising processes; but they also raise interesting theoretical questions in themselves. Indeed nothing undermines the plausibility of the 'civilising process' thesis more than the widespread perception that, whatever may have been the trend in Europe from the Middle Ages to the nineteenth century, the present century has seen a reversal in many of those trends. A major debate took place among Dutch sociologists about whether the advent of 'the permissive society' in the 1960s and 1970s—particularly dramatic in the Netherlands—meant that the long-term European civilising process had at last gone into reverse, and whether this falsified Elias's theory.[19] A parallel debate among British sociologists—and the wider public—has concerned the apparent upturn since the 1960s in the incidence of violence in the United Kingdom. That was the context in which Eric Dunning and his colleagues were led to remark that 'we do not fully understand the periodicity and ups and downs, . . . the conditions under which a society moves, on balance, in a "civilising" direction and the conditions under which a civilising process moves, as it were, on balance into "reverse gear" ' (1988: 243). This observation seems to have general historical validity, and it is one of the key problems for further research.

To help clarify the issues involved I shall distinguish between short-term and long-term decivilising processes, according to whether decivilising trends become dominant for a relatively short period or for a period of at least three generations. For an example of the first, let us turn to the Nazi period in Germany.

The Holocaust. Sir Edmund Leach (1986) alleged that at the very time that Elias was formulating his thesis, 'Hitler was refuting the argument on the grandest scale'. Elias, it is true, completed *The Civilising Process* before the 'final solution' had taken final form, but something of the character of the Nazi regime was already clear. In fact, he explained in the preface, 'the issues raised by the book have their origins less in scholarly tradition, in the narrower sense of the word, than in the experiences in whose shadow we all live, experiences of the crisis and transformation of Western civilisation as it has existed hitherto . . .' (1939: I, xvii). While he, like virtually everyone else, no doubt failed to foresee the extent of the killings, a sense of foreboding is occasionally evident. For example, explaining that the control of dangers gradually established in society was a precondition for the 'civilised' standard of conduct, he added that

> The armour of civilised conduct would crumble very rapidly if, through a change in society, the degree of insecurity that existed earlier were to break in upon us again, and if danger became as incalculable as once it was. Corresponding fears would burst the limits set to them today. (1939: I, 307n).

In other words, civilised conduct takes a long time to construct, but can be destroyed rather quickly. That, I think, is one of the central problems of the whole theory: at first glance, Elias appears to want to have his cake and eat it too.

However, some points drawn both from Elias's own thinking and from game theory may help to explain the apparent asymmetry at which Elias is hinting. First, it must be remembered that, though standards change from generation to generation in the course of a social learning process extending over many lifetimes, the prevalent standards of controls at any point in the process have to be acquired—or not acquired—by every individual in every generation through an individual learning process, by definition no longer than an individual lifetime. Abrupt changes in social circumstances may seriously disrupt the continuity of socialisation.

Furthermore, such changes may indeed bring about changes in behaviour in periods much shorter than an individual lifetime, without enough time having elapsed for changes in socialisation to have taken place. For it must be remembered that Elias thinks of civilising processes as involving a change in the *balance* between *Fremdzwänge* (external contraints, constraints *by other people*) and *Selbstzwänge* (self-constraints)—the balance tilting towards the latter in the control of behaviour in the average person, but without constraints-by-others ever ceasing to operate. The operation of self-constraints will not remain unchanged if changes take place in the patterning of external constraints—the behaviour of other people. Calculation of the external constraints always plays a part in the steering of conduct, and if the calculations suddenly or gradually yield different outcomes, behaviour will change. Still more will it change if the outcomes become—as Elias says in the remark just quoted—more *in*calculable: the pattern of people's *fears* responds to changes in the *dangers* they face. And one of the distinguishing characteristics of decivilising trends is a rise in the level of danger and a fall in its calculability.

This makes sense in game theoretic terms too. Changes in contraints-by-others can equally well be thought of as changes in the structure of games in which people are involved, and in the feasible sets they face. It certainly makes sense that if one is no longer so confident that one's opponent will act according to calculable standards of self-constraint, one's own self-constraints may weigh less heavily in the balance of one's own conduct. Decivilising episodes typically involve people's feasible sets contracting in some directions (no longer safe to depend on the security of some outcomes . . .) and expanding in others (greater chances of getting away with other strategies . . .). Changed behaviour in such circumstances is no shock to the theory of decivilising processes, because it does not rest simply on 'binding social norms'. The theory also points to some of the directions in which behaviour may change.

It is not wise to try to use the theory of civilising processes to explain *everything* that happens in a case like Nazi Germany, where a group of people seizes power and threatens for a time to lower the whole level of 'civilisation' in the technical sense. Many other sociologists and historians have written in more detail than Elias about the roots of nationalistic and particularistic ideologies in Germany and about how the strains of defeat and economic crisis after 1918 assisted in the rise of Nazism.[20] All the same, Elias's ideas are particularly helpful in seeking an answer to what often seems the most puzzling question of all, 'Why did so many ordinary, decent Germans stand by and allow persecution and genocide to happen?'

Part of the answer appears to lie in the unintended aggregate effects of many individuals leading their own humdrum lives, with short-term interests predominating over any wider picture. Christabel Bielenberg has captured with very great subtlety the changes brought about in many ordinary people's relations with their Jewish acquaintances by the inception of persecution, and how shortsightedness could be combined with that most mundane of Elias's forms of foresight: embarrassment.

> The Nuremberg Laws, for instance, most certainly provided some Jews and also some Gentiles with just that flash of insight needed to show them that the writing was on the wall and the exodus must begin; they did not do so

for me. I could pinpoint no exact date when normal and natural association with Jewish friends became an act of defiance and then petered out, not because the friend was less close, but simply because such a relationship is an unnatural one; mutual embarrassment intervenes. At first we were no less credulous than they. Why should they go? The whole thing was crazy—couldn't possibly last. When was it that credulity turned to doubt, doubt to resignation, and to the unhappy, rather shamefaced admission that you were very sorry, you could not help it, you happened to have been labelled an Aryan (whatever that might be), and truth to tell you'd be mighty relieved to know that the good friend was safely off your conscience overseas? (Bielenberg, 1968: 30)

In any case, times of crisis are not conducive to taking the longer view, nor a relatively detached view. Elias's notion of the triad of controls is relevant in understanding the appeal of (literally) fantastic beliefs. During times of social crisis—military defeats, political revolutions, rampant inflation, soaring unemployment, separately or in combination—fears rise because control of social events has declined. Rising fears make it still more difficult to control events. That makes people still more susceptible to wish fantasies about means of alleviating the situation. A vicious circle or 'double-bind process' is set up, and a process of that kind can be clearly seen in Germany after 1918, helping to explain the rise of the Nazis and the appeal of racial beliefs.[21]

While Elias associates the emergence of larger and larger survival units with the growth of a generally wider sense of mutual identification, he always stresses that this sense is felt much more weakly towards members of other survival units, and towards outsider groups[22] within one's own survival group. The Jews had, of course, always been an outsider group; there had always been anti-semitism in Germany, although it is easy with hindsight to exaggerate its extent. It is striking how hard the Nazi regime had to strive to diminish the identification which many Germans—in spite of the mechanism of drifting acquiescence described by Christabel Bielenberg—felt with their fellow-Germans, the Jews (which was evident, for instance, in the popular reaction to *Kristallnacht*, 1938). It was not merely a matter of propaganda, whipping up a sense of danger. The Jews were first removed to ghettos, breaking their personal contacts with their non-Jewish neighbours. Then, under the official pretext of 'resettlement in the east', they were removed to transit camps, labour camps, and finally extermination camps to some extent 'behind the scenes' at least of metropolitan Germany. The regime remained apprehensive of German public opinion even at this stage (on all this, see Noakes and Pridham, 1988: III, 997–1208). 'Mutual identification' was apparently not something that could be ignored, but we are still left with the vast sociological, and moral, question of why it was so relatively easily by-passed.

Paradoxically, the social relations between prisoners in the extreme conditions of the camps themselves show something of the connection between the shortening of foresight and the decline of mutual identification. Primo Levi wrote with unparalleled vividness of what it was like to be forced to live with the overriding short-term objective of surviving until the next day. And though his books were written as witness to the memory of his many friends who died and all his fellow prisoners who suffered with him, he is candid about the generally limited sense of mutual identification among inmates at the time:

> There was little feeling of *camaraderie* among us. It was confined to compatriots, and even toward them it was weakened by the minimal life conditions. It was actually zero, indeed negative, with regard to newcomers. In this and many other respects we had greatly retrogressed and become hardened. And in the 'new' fellow prisoner we tended to see an alien, an oafish, cumbersome barbarian who took up space, time, and bread, who did not know the unspoken but ironclad rules of coexistence, and who, moreover, complained (and for the wrong reasons) in an irritating and ridiculous manner . . . (Levi, 1987: 67)

A final way that the theory of civilising processes casts light on the Holocaust is still more grimly paradoxical. Modern social organisation vastly multiplied the technical capacity to kill. The very long chains of interdependence and 'division of social functions' which play such a part in the civilising process were also essential to implementing the 'final solution'. And ironically, as Elias argues, 'civilised' controls in turn play their part in making possible those long chains of organised and co-ordinated activities. Many of these chains had been violently shaken by military defeat in 1918, and were to be again in 1945, but on the whole they remained intact during the Nazi period—and that is what distinguishes this sort of short-term decivilising episode from the longer-term processes to be considered next. In many ways, it is a more complex problem to explain why decivilising trends should become only temporarily dominant than it is to explain the decivilising consequences of longer-term social disintegration.

The Holocaust refuted the theory of the European civilising process in much the same way that the Black Death cast doubt on the long-term tendency for the continent's population to grow. That is not facetious, nor an attempt to immunise the theory against falsification. The fact is that, for all the horrific suffering the Holocaust involved, civilising tendencies regained dominance after a relatively few years; whether and how they would have done so without external military intervention we can only speculate.

Decivilising Processes over Several Generations. By longer-term decivilising processes I mean those which continued over at least three generations. I specify that length of time because that, it seems to me, is the minimum period over which one could hope to be able to observe whether the changes in the socialisation process—to which Elias drew attention as the means by which changing standards of civilised controls were transmitted from generation to generation—actually go into reverse when structures are broken and danger levels rise.[23]

The most significant questions that may be asked about these longer-term decivilising processes fall into two main groups, corresponding more or less to the questions uppermost respectively in the second and first volumes of Elias's original discussion of civilising processes. The first group of questions are 'structural': in what circumstances do the chains of interdependence in society begin to break, and thus why do levels of complexity, differentiation and integration start to decline? The second group concerns the outcome of such processes of structural unravelling for people's experience: what are the cultural and psychological consequences and the impact on people's day-to-day conduct?

There is a third set of questions which is not negligible. That relates to the possible loss of certain learned psychological qualities and behavioural capacities—primarily, in the context of our discussion, any tilting of the balance back away from self-constraints, any associated decline in the general capacity for detour behaviour and the exercise of foresight, and any decline in the breadth of mutual identification. Just as, according to Elias, the acquisition of these 'civilised' capacities played a part in the development of more complex forms of social organisation, so their loss may contribute in turn to structural decline once it has started. For centuries, writers who have meditated on the causes of the downfall of states and empires have dwelt on symptoms of 'moral decline' as they saw it. In such cases as that of Ancient Rome, modern historians would at least want to ask whether their predecessors did not confuse cause and effect. Elias's theory points to the likelihood that these changes would occur in response to a rise in levels of danger and a decline in the calculability of social life, consequent on structural decline. But, as we have argued, there is no need to adopt a monocausal, unidirectional theory in attempting to explain decivilisation as a *process*. I shall, however, dwell here mainly on the first two groups of question.

The most spectacular instances of decivilising processes extending over several generations are the cases of more or less total collapse of complex societies, of which Tainter (1988) gives a surprisingly long list. They include the Western Chou empire in China, the Mesopotamian empires, the Egyptian Old Kingdom, the Hittite empire, the Minoan civilisation, the Western Roman Empire, and several of the pre-Columbian New World empires. (Some of these were not especially complex by modern standards of complexity.) In my view, however, it makes sense not to study cases of near-total collapse alone, but also cases of perhaps temporary weakening and resurgence of centrifugal forces followed not by collapse but by relative stagnation or eventually resumed economic and political growth. Only by comparing the two sorts of case can we begin to generalise about how effectively the shock absorbers typically work in complex societies of various kinds. Both cases may bring decivilising trends into dominance.

Tainter provides a careful eleven-fold categorisation and critique of earlier explanations of collapse. The effects of bureaucratic empires acting as revenue pumps, on which Jones lays some stress as obstacles to a transition from extensive to intensive growth, come in for criticism from Tainter if they are extended to use as an explanation of general socio-political collapse.

> Elite mismanagement and self-aggrandisement, to the extent that they are detrimental to the survival of a society, are matters to be explained. Exploitation and mismanagement are normal, regular aspects of complex societies, and by themselves cannot account for an occasional event, collapse. (1988: 89; cf. 64–73)

Tainter's own favoured explanation of collapse, however, has some-thing in common with Jones's argument here. It is essentially economic, though extended to contexts that are not narrowly economic, and depends on a generalisation of the economists' notion of declining marginal product. Collapse comes about because 'investment in socio-political complexity often reaches a point of declining marginal returns' (1988: 118). By returns he means 'benefits to people'. *Which* people is an issue not fully explored, but by implication refers mainly to powerful elite groups; here again there is a point of similarity with Jones's thinking (and also, incidentally, with De Swaan's).

Tainter's argument is that the creation and maintenance of large-scale, geographically extensive, highly differentiated societies requires ever-increasing investment in agriculture and resource production, in overall economic productivity, in information processing, and in 'socio-political control and specialisation'. This last is a key point, raising the same 'interplay of control and dependency' to which Goudsblom (pages 21-2 above) draws attention. In each of these fields, diminishing marginal returns are likely to set in:

> To maintain growth in complexity, hierarchies levy taxes on their popula-tions. At some point even this yields declining marginal returns. This happens when rates are so high that tax avoidance increases and taxation-induced inflation erodes the value of the money collected. (Tainter, 1988: 116)

Investment is required not only for administrative co-ordination, defence and so forth, but also for 'legitimation activities'—doles, bread and circuses etc.—but each successive increase of expenditure soon becomes the expected level and the marginal returns in legitimacy diminish. The principle applies equally to investment in the main alternative means of maintaining order, the means of coercion.

The main weakness of Tainter's theory, however, is that his illustra-tions of the diminishing marginal returns of complexity are 'un-convincingly dire glosses on production costs in the world today' (Jones, 1989b). When he applies it historically, Tainter has difficulty in specifying the point at which diminishing returns set in—independently, that is, of collapse itself. The theory therefore has a somewhat *ex post facto* quality. It appears chiefly to redescribe the problem—though in usefully more general terms, so it is not devoid of cognitive value.

In fact, we seem still not to have any general theory of social collapse.

Perhaps it is not sensible to look for one. For not only are precipitating circumstances possibly too varied to be effectively subsumed under a higher-level abstraction like 'diminishing marginal returns', but the cases of collapse with which Tainter is concerned are in the tail of the distribution of a broader class of events including the frustration of tendencies to growth and periods when centrifugal forces become only temporarily dominant.

The chances of fruitful generalisation may, it seems to me, be greater in relation to my second group of questions concerning the cultural and psychological effects and the impact on people's conduct when 'structural unravelling' occurs in various forms and degrees. What are the consequences of such more or less long-term processes for people's pursuit of more or less short-term interests through their day-to-day experience? Here again, Axelrod's evolutionary theory of co-operation is suggestive in thinking about the apparent asymmetry between gradual civilising and more rapid decivilising processes. His experimental studies of sequential games point to the conclusion that co-operation can begin with small clusters of people, and it thrives when people follow strategies that are 'nice, provocable, and somewhat forgiving' (such as tit-for-tat). Once such strategies of reciprocity are well established, a group of people using them can protect itself even from a cluster of individuals who try to exploit the rest. 'The overall level of co-operation tends to go up and not down. In other words, *the machinery for the evolution of co-operation contains a ratchet*' (Axelrod, 1984: 177, my italics). The reason is that:

> Once word gets out that reciprocity works, it becomes the thing to do. If you expect others to reciprocate your defections as well as your co-operations, you will be wise to avoid starting any trouble. Moreover, you will be wise to defect after someone else defects, showing that you will not be exploited. Thus you too will be wise to use a strategy based on reciprocity. So will everyone else. In this manner the appreciation of the value of reciprocity becomes self-reinforcing. Once it gets going, it gets stronger and stronger. (1984: 189)

That does not directly lead to a simple explanation of how large a shock is necessary to send the process into reverse. But Axelrod's experiments led him to the view that 'the foundation of co-operation is not really trust but the durability of the relationship', and that 'for co-operation to prove stable, the future must have a sufficiently large shadow' (1984: 182, 174). Expectations of future interdependence are crucial (as Elias pointed out in his discussion of the behaviour of courtiers). Furthermore, it is when this anticipation of future inter-dependence breaks down that—in the experiments—an external authority is invoked. In many of the real-world historical examples with which we are concerned, however, the decline of external authority was itself one of the main causes of the breakdown of that anticipation.

An increase in levels of danger and incalculability, and a decline in the capacity of central governments to enforce their authority, will be associated with the re-emergence of free rider problems. The con-sequence will be the onset of disinvestment in collective goods. Looked at from the point of view of the more or less short-term interests of individual people and small groups, it simply becomes less safe than formerly to depend on people at a distance down fracturing chains. Collective arrangements which ultimately rested on the capacity of authorities to enforce them can no longer be relied upon. De Swaan's collectivising process goes into reverse, and in this gearbox the reverse gears may well be of higher ratios than the forward ones. One economic principle not used by Tainter may be a useful analogy here: the accelerator (or, in this context, decelerator) mechanism. It is well known that when rates of investment decline, or even merely slow down, it has magnified knock-on effects on levels of activity in the wider economy. In periods when the chains of social interdependence are breaking, people disinvest in collective goods at an accelerating rate. Sometimes this can happen startlingly quickly; Tainter (1988: 19) mentions the abrupt collapse of order in Istanbul after the disintegration of Turkish authority in 1918, with public transport at a standstill, corpses left unburied, and the police turning to banditry. In other cases, such as Beirut in the 1970s and 1980s, the process may be delayed but then occur quite suddenly. For more than decade after the onset of the highly destructive Lebanese civil war, commerce was maintained with sur-prising normality in a divided and besieged city; yet when finally it collapsed, the collapse occurred quickly. This delay could be explained, perhaps, as the effect of adjustment costs which people were not willing to incur until they were quite sure the changes were not going to be quickly reversed.

In the space of a generation or two, smaller and less dense webs of interdependence entailing fewer pressures towards foresight and self-constraint in the co-ordination of activities may, through the socialisation process, result in diminution of these capacities. People need to practice them if they are to be able to call on them at will. Conversely, in situations of greater insecurity, learning aptitudes resting on a very different temperament may have greater survival value.

In studying the psychological and cultural components of this process in historical contexts, contemporary studies of the effects of increased levels of violence on adults and children in places like Northern Ireland and the Lebanon (Cairns and Wilson; 1985, Hosin, 1983) ought to be relevant. Increased levels of danger ought to be associated with increased fear and anxiety, and with a lessening of controls.[24] As always, in practice it is not easy to make inferences from short-term studies to long-term trends. The increase in anxiety shows up in Northern Ireland, but as realistic, not neurotic anxiety. On the other hand, it may be thought that the relatively high level of inter-communal conflict in Northern Ireland over many generations is reflected in the rather high fantasy content of popular beliefs in the province (see MacDonald, 1983). But applying such insights to historical evidence is quite difficult, in part because periods of social disintegration are times when documentary evidence is likely to be less complete and clear.

The task of disentangling economic, political and cultural strands of causality in a case such as the decline of Rome is immense. Max Weber stressed one basic point:

> the civilisation of Antiquity did not decline because the Empire fell, for the Roman Empire as a political structure existed for centuries after ancient civilisation had passed its prime. In fact this civilisation had been in eclipse for a long time. By the early third century Roman literature was played out, and Roman jurisprudence deteriorated together with its schools. Greek and Latin poetry were moribund, historiography faded away, and even inscriptions started to fall silent. Latin itself soon gave way to dialects.
>
> When, after one and half centuries of decline, the Western Empire finally disappeared, barbarism had already conquered the Empire from within. (Weber, 1896: 389)

Weber goes on to make clear that by 'the civilisation of Antiquity'[25] he means primarily *urban* culture, and in the decline of towns, economic and political forces certainly played a major part, even while the Western

Empire persisted. Even so, the picture is complex. Weber's argument brings out once more that decivilising processes involve civilising components, as well as *vice versa*. Emphasising the part played by the decline of slavery in the decline of ancient culture, Weber shows how, including as it did the transformation of slaves into serfs living not in barracks but in cottages with their own families, this involved an *increase* in mutual identification:

> What we have described was a transformation of the fundamental structures of society, a transformation which was necessary and which must be interpreted as a tremendous process of recovery.[26] For the great masses of unfree people regained family life and private property, and they themselves were elevated from the status 'speaking tools' to the plane of humanity. Ascendant Christianity now surrounded their family life with firm moral guarantees; indeed even the laws of the Later Empire for the protection of peasants' rights acknowledged the unity of the unfree family to an unprecedented degree.
>
> It is also of course true that at the same time a part of the unfree population sank to a position equivalent to sefdom, and the civilised aristocracy of Antiquity was barbarised. (Weber, 1896: 410)

All this serves as a reminder that one should not expect everything suggested in the right hand column of our table to show up in a mechanical and linear way. The coexistence of civilising and decivilising trends certainly complicates the problem of interpretation. For example, Tainter (1988: 6) points out that the classical flowering of Chinese culture took place precisely in the aftermath of the collapse of the Western Chou. But this is less surprising than it seems at first glance. For the period of the Warring States (*c.* 400–221 BC) which followed the Chou, like the period of the 'elimination contest' in medieval Europe, was for all its turbulence one in which centripetal, integrating forces were in the ascendant, with gradual centralisation of power and the formation of great courts; and some of the socio-cultural developments of that period in China bear a resemblance to those in Europe a millennium and a half later documented by Elias (cf. Gernet, 1982: 62–100).

As I have already argued, the study of decivilising processes over several generations need not be confined to cases of final and unreversed total collapse. Cases where subsequent recovery occurred are also relevant. For instance the Thirty Years War had a prolonged effect on German life and culture for several generations before the recovery in the eighteenth century (cf. Langer, 1981; Sagarra 1977). Contemporaries depict a coarsening of manners and culture which persisted for some time, quite apart from the material, economic and political consequences of the war. Another interesting case may prove to be the Wild West, ironically because opinion among historians emphasises how relatively well social order and 'civilised behaviour' held up. (One must not forget, though, that the extent of mutual identification was in general not sufficiently wide to include the Indians—but then one would not expect it to be as strong across the boundary of a state society.) But the relatively high persistence of 'civilised' standards is what makes the case interesting. When people migrate into an area where the state apparatus is, at least temporarily, less effective, where the strength of *Fremdzwänge* is less and danger levels are higher, they themselves have generally been socialised in conditions where this was not the case. So, if the Wild West was not all that wild, it may throw some light on humans' capacity to 'run on their batteries' of self-constraints for some time. And that in turn may throw some light on the dynamics of a situation—like the decline of the Roman Empire—where the rise in the danger level was not a merely short-term blip.

4. Conclusion

In this chapter I have tried to do several things at once. In taking up the relationship between short-term interests and long-term processes, I have looked for areas of complementarity between a 'process-sociology' of Eliasian stamp on the one hand and economic/rational-choice theory on the other—outwardly two unpromisingly dissimilar approaches. What I have written is unashamedly exploratory and programmatic, and many issues are left unresolved. For instance, the part played by 'increasing mutual identification' in the growth of social complexity needs further thought. One aspect of it at least, 'mutually expected self-constraints' in Goudsblom's phrase, appears consonant with the findings of games theorists. More generally, theories of choice and games theory can yield insight into how people pursue their more or less short-term interests in the course of more or less long-term processes—even though such theories have so far paid little attention to long-term processes. On the other hand, rational choice theory (and economic theory) has worked with the most primitive of psychological assumptions, centring on the most basic and unchanging of human capacities for rational action. How personality and the patterning of rationality are themselves changed in the course of social development—a central concern of Elias's—is entirely neglected. But, tentatively, we can conclude that the two approaches together are likely to prove useful in discovering the structure involved in 'decivilising' processes. And it is the common contention of the three authors of this book that long-term processes are *structured*: the search for structure in long-term processes is what prevents our endeavours yielding only one-thing-after-another history.

Notes

Introduction: Bringing the Very Long Term back in

1. For a full discussion of Norbert Elias's notion of 'process theories' and their place in his theory of knowledge, see Mennell, 1989a: 176–81, 252–8, 274–5n. As Goudsblom implies in Note 3 to Chapter 1 below, William McNeill has independently reached a similar conception of process theories as the aim of historical research; see his book *Mythistory and Other Essays* (McNeill, 1986: 43–67).

2. The phrase is Elias's (1987b). Goudsblom (1977: 7) has coined the useful word 'hodiecentrism' (by comparison with 'ethnocentrism') to designate the today-centred thinking of so much modern sociology.

3. I have developed this argument at greater length in my paper 'The Sociological Study of History: Institutions and Social Development' (Mennell, 1989b).

4. For a discussion of 'functionalism' and its relation to evolutionary theories, see Mennell, 1974: 141–67.

5. For a defence of developmental sociology against the claims of Popper, see Dunning (1977).

6. See the Supplementary Bibliographical Guide in the second edition of Jones's *The European Miracle* (1987: 272–4).

7. The notion of the *longue durée* was sufficient to earn the *Annales* school a chapter by Stuart Clark (1985) in Quentin Skinner's collection *The Return of Grand Theory in the Social Sciences*.

8. In a recent paper (1989) and a forthcoming book (1990), Stephen K. Sanderson argues for what he calls 'evolutionism without developmentalism'. Although I entirely agree with his argument—he is pursuing a non-teleological, non-unilinear form of what I would call developmental theory—he uses the two words 'evolutionism' and 'developmentalism' in precisely the opposite sense to our usage. That is, I think, because Nisbet (1969) made 'developmentalism' a dirty word among American sociologists, whereas in the world of British anthropology and sociology the same connotations have remained attached to 'evolutionism'. The nomenclature is confusing, but in the underlying argument there is no disagreement.

9. See my discussion of cultural relativism and anthropological arguments

against Elias's theories (Mennell, 1989a: 227–41). See especially Elias (1989).

Chapter One: Human History and Long-Term Social Proceses

1. See McNeill 1986. I prefer the term 'human history' to 'world history', since the latter, strictly speaking, refers to the history of the world as a geological process. This may, however, reflect a hypersensitivity to the literal meaning of words that is sometimes exhibited by non-native English speakers.
2. Cf. Elias, 1989; see also Hallpike 1986 for a clear distinction between social and biological evolution. See also Stephen Mennell's remark in Note 8 to the Introduction above.
3. Cf. Elias 1977; see also McNeill's essay, 1986: 43–67.

Chapter Two: Extensive Growth in The Premodern World

1. A preliminary version of this argument appears in E.L. Jones (1982).
2.. See the annual *World Development Reports* of the World Bank for statistics on growth performance.
3. For estimates of the rates of capital formation in certain premodern economies, see Goldsmith, 1987: 36, 101, 132-133, 202-203.
4. Rozman, 1973: 6; Chandler and Fox, 1974. The comment by Jan de Vries (1984: 18) that the Chandler and Fox data are 'all but unusable' is a little severe given our very general purposes.
5. I am grateful to Professor Taagepera for copies of his working papers.
6. See especially the first chapter of Elvin 1973.
7. As demonstrated in a forthcoming La Trobe University Ph.D thesis by my student, Zhou Linong.
8. Calculated from Taagepera 1978: Table 6.
9. The Roman empire is exquisitely placed in context, and to some extent cut down to its proper relative size, in Sitwell, 1986.
10. They have not however responded persuasively to the challenge by J.L. Anderson, 1981. See for instance Galloway, 1986, 'Long-term Fluctuations in Climate and Population in the Preindustrial Era', *Population and Development Review* 12:1–24.
11. The difficulties of raising output were exaggerated in the development literature of the 1950s, 60s and 70s, two characteristics of which were its short-period focus and, seen in historical perspective, wanting all change overnight.
12. See the treatment by Crosby, 1986.

Chapter Three: Recurrent Transitions to Intensive Growth

1. See McCormack, 1988: 3–4.
2. Maddison (1982) makes clear the sequence of changes in world economic leadership.
3. There is a clever argument for the independent role of spatial arrangements in social change in Dodgshon, 1987, but this does not refer directly to configurations of natural resources.

Chapter Four: Ecological Regimes and The Rise of Organised Religion

1. As Gellner observes in the opening paragraphs of *Plough, Sword and Book* (1988: 11): 'Men and societies frequently treat the institutions and assumptions by which they live as absolute, self-evident, and given. They may treat them as such without question, or they may endeavour to fortify them by some kind of proof. In fact, human ideas and social forms are neither static nor given.'
2. Tylor, 1871. See also Harris, 1968: 201–7.
3. So far, two of my papers on the subject have been published in English (Goudsblom, 1986, 1987). For a more extended discus,sion of the initial stages in the domestication process see also the first two instalments of the series of articles in Dutch on 'Fire and Civilisation' (Goudsblom, 1984–88). See also the literature cited there and, in addition, Clark and Harris (1985), Perlès (1987) and James (1989). The degree to which the domestication of fire was a pre-condition for agrarianisation and continued to play a part in agrarian societies is dealt with in the successive instalments of the Dutch series of articles.
4. Writers who have alerted me to this problem include (apart from Weber, 1922) McNeill (1963), Lenski (1966), Harris (1977), and especially Elias (1939). More recently I have come across the monographs by Glassman (1986) and Gellner (1988) which also deal incisively with the rise to power of priests.
5. The trifold formulation is by Talcott Parsons. See Goudsblom, 1960: 69.
6. 'One should . . . not be surprised to find that these leisured priests-elders would increase their skills and knowledge in manipulating people and use it to elevate further their own position so that they would emerge as the first aristocracy, the first upper class, the first ruling stratum'. Glassman (1986: II, 33).
7. Thus, to give just a few examples, Gerhard Lenski, one of the few sociologists who have addressed the problem of priestly rule as a general

problem of social stratification, defines priests as 'those who mediate in the relation between God, or the gods, and man in the performance of holy rites' (Lenski 1966: 256). Likewise Norbert Elias, who cannot possibly be suspected of theological leanings and who has insisted even more strongly than Lenski that the problem is to be seen as one of social power, writes that 'the power of priests was derived in the first place from their special relationship with the gods' (Elias 1987: 241). In a similar vein Johnson and Earle write in their excellent monograph on the evolution of human societies: 'Descended from gods and invested with special powers, the chief has the final say in all matters involving the group, including ceremonies, adjucations, war, and diplomacy' (Johnson and Earle 1987: 318). From an archæological atlas I quote: 'The administrative demands of the growing population led to the rise of bureaucracies and encouraged the adoption of writing. Professional priestly classes came into being to regulate relations with the gods' (*Past Worlds* 1988: 103); 'Each city (in Mesopotamia) was under the protection of a particular god, housed in the splendidly fitted main temple along with his numerous human retinue' (*id.*: 124). Finally, to conclude this arbitrary collection: 'Yet always beneath both Mexica patriotism and the rational goals of the state were the insatiable demands of the gods. The pantheon's need for an ever greater number of sacrificial offerings required unceasing warfare to obtain captives' (Conrad and Demarest 1984: 44).
8. See for example Boserup, 1965; Sahlins, 1972.
9. In the concepts 'ecological regime' and 'agrarian regime' as I use them here the meaning of the word 'regime' is not confined to the common dictionary definition of 'mode of rule' or 'prevailing governmental system'. My use of the term 'agrarian regime' is compatible with Marc Bloch's view that 'Each [agrarian] regime is an intricate complex of techniques and social relations' (1966: 35). The term is intended to refer to a concept of the same order as the concept of 'medical regime' as developed by De Swaan (1988) and 'religious regime' as developed by Bax (1988), both of which are elaborations upon Elias's (1939) theory of the interplay of 'internal' and 'external' constraints.

Chapter Five: The Formation of Military-Agrarian Regimes

1. On Hesiod, see West 1978. A highly readable translation of *Works and Days* is that by Dorothea Wender, Harmondsworth, Penguin Books, 1973.
2. Homer, *Odyssey* IX:39–43. Prose translation by E.V. Rieu, Harmondsworth, Penguin Books, 1946.
3. Cf. Elias, 1970: 261–63; Goudsblom, 1977: 126–31.

4. See also Clastres 1980: 171–248. As Wolf (1982) and others point out, both the wars themselves and the way in which they were fought are to be seen in relation to the pressures exerted by European colonists. Their influence on the American Indians may be compared to the impact of the Romans on the Germanic tribes in Northern Europe in the first centuries of the Christian era. The rise of religious leaders in times of military adversity such as the North American Indians went through is discussed by Wilson (1975).

5. On monopolisation of military force, see Elias, 1939: 91–228. It is important to note that the monopolisation of military force, first by men, and then by a class of professional warriors, necessarily preceded the centralisation of the monopoly in the process of state formation as described by Elias.

6. The indications for Mesopotamia include Wenke, 1984: 249–67; those for China, *id.*, 325–27 and Stover and Stover 1977: 25, 38; those for Meso-america, Conrad and Demarest, 1984: 19 and (with some reservations) 88. While evidence for the historic priority of a 'theocracy' (as rule by priests is conventionally but somewhat misleadingly called) appears to be less strong than earlier writers such as Adams (1966) and Wolf (1959) have concluded, the case for such priority has still been stated persuasively by Glassman (1986: II, 25–34).

7. The non-teleological way in which the concept of 'functions' is used here is further discussed in Goudsblom, 1977: 175–80.

8. See Hall, 1985; Jones 1987, 1988; and Mann, 1986. Armed struggles between peasants and warrior groups possessing a monopoly of superior military force have continued from the days of the Assyrians well into the twentieth century. A typical testimony of the power balances in such confrontations may be found in Winston Churchill's memoirs of his years as a military officer in India. His account of an expedition against the Pathans reads like an echo of the memoirs of Julius Caesar and other great military commanders:

> 'Sir Bindon sent orders that we were to stay in the Mamud valley and lay it waste with fire and sword in vengeance. This accordingly we did, with great precautions. We proceeded systematically, village by village, and we destroyed the houses, filled up the wells, blew down the towers, cut down the great shady trees, burned the crops and broke the reservoirs in punitive devastation' (1930: 162).

Accounts such as this provide the background for Churchill's observation that the British government in India was 'patient because among other things it knows that if the worst comes to the worst, it can shoot anybody down' (1930: 148). Churchill's statesmanship is expressed in the words:

'So societies in quiet years should be constructed; overwhelming force on the side of the rulers, innumerable objections to the use of any part of it' (id.).
9. Friedrich Nietzsche, 'On the Genealogy of Morals' (1887) in Kaufmann 1968: 439–602.
10. Weber 1922: I, 526–76. On the harshness of social relations in Rome see Hopkins (1978) and MacMullen (1974). On the Aztecs, see Conrad and Demarest (1984).

Chapter Six: Short-Term Interests and Long-Term Processes

1. This paper grew out of work begun while I held a Nuffield Foundation Social Science Research Fellowship (1986-88) and a Fellowship at the Netherlands Institute for Advanced Study, Wassenaar; I wish to acknowledge the support of both institutions. I should also like to thank the following friends and colleagues who have commented on earlier versions of the chapter: Peter Abell, Jonathan Barry, Ian Hampsher-Monk, Helen Hintjens, John Goldthorpe, and of course Joop Goudsblom and Eric Jones. With such a diverse group, offering in some cases quite contradictory advice, the usual disclaimer applies more strongly than ever: final responsibility is entirely my own.
2. My interest in decivilising processes in fact arises out of criticisms that have been made of Elias's theory of long-term civilising processes. The four principal lines of criticism are:
    1. Criticisms from the viewpoint of cultural relativism;
    2. Criticisms from the argument that there are 'stateless civilisations'.
    3. The argument from the 'permissive society'; and
    4. The 'barbarisation' argument.
   The first two lines of criticism emanate especially from anthropologists. It is the third and fourth criticisms which raise the most interesting questions in relation to the problem of direction. They have in common that they are both concerned with apparent reversals in the main trend of the process Elias traces through European history, and appear to cast doubt on the validity of his explanation of that process. Here I concentrate on the fourth issue; I have dealt with the other three at length elsewhere (Mennell, 1989a: 227–46).
3. In fact, especially in his more recent works such as *Über die Zeit* (1984) and *Humana Conditio* (1985), Elias has spoken of civilising processes on a third level, that of humanity as a whole. The distinction is explained most clearly by Goudsblom (1984); see also Mennell (1989a: 200–24). Goudsblom's own work on the domestication of fire (1987) and his

chapters in this volume proceed at this third level, and it could be argued that Eric Jones's focus is also on processes at the level of humanity as a whole. At this stage, however, my own interests in the social psychological and cultural components of decivilising processes lie in the other two levels explained in the text.

4. For a more detailed discussion, see Mennell (1989a), especially chapter 4.

5. See Stone and Mennell, 1980: 40, 102–6.

6. Cf. Goudsblom, page 71 above.

7. I use the plural as a reminder that this is true not just of the European civilising process originally discussed by Elias, but also, as for example Goudsblom shows in his work on the domestication of fire and his discussions of agrarianisation in this volume, of many other contexts too.

8. For a somewhat fuller discussion of traditional sociological theories in this light, see Mennell, 1974: 116–40.

9. Rational choice theory is itself most closely related to the 'exchange' tradition, yet the game theoretic branch of it radically undermines any easy assumption that reciprocity leads automatically to the common advantage. See Coleman's essay 'Beyond Pareto Optimality', 1986: 33–62.

10. Olson offers a formal proof of his theorem in the first chapter of his book (1965: 5–52), and in subsequent chapters adduces a good deal of empirical evidence to support it. Here I am merely drawing on his own summary of the thesis given in the Introduction, pp. 1–3.

11. Olson conceded that none of this applied fully to small groups, which are more complicated. The difference between large and small groups was analogous to that between situations of perfect and monopolistic competition. In small groups, there might be some collusive action in support of the common purposes of the individuals in the group, but this would generally cease before it reached the optimal level for members of the group as a whole. More recent work (e.g. Oliver and Marwell, 1988) has substantially qualified Olson's thesis, especially the distinction between large and small groups: much in fact depends on whether the costs of public goods rise with the number who share them. Nevertheless, this work does nothing to diminish, and if anything serves to increase, the complexity of the problem of how groups achieve collective attention without coercion. From a different angle, Elias drew attention to the complexity of possible lines of alliance and cleavage in even quite small groups in the calculations given in his 'Index of Complexity' (1970: 101).

12. Elias was then of course writing before the emergence of rational choice theory in its modern form, before even the publication of Von Neumann and Morgenstern's *Theory of Games and Economic Behaviour* (1944). Much later, however, while teaching at the University of Leicester during the 1950s and 1960s, he developed his series of (non-mathematical) 'Game

Models' based in good part on the 'elimination contest' between warriors, and on the forms of oligarchic competition depicted in *The Court Society*. These Game Models are to be found in Elias's book *What is Sociology?* (orig. 1970), and they could well have been partly inspired not only by Von Neumann and Morgenstern but by books such as Luce and Raiffa's *Games and Decisions* (1957) and Rapoport's *Fights, Games and Debates* (1960).

13. Wrong's critique was directed at Talcott Parsons. Jon Elster (1986), in a complementary critique of what he calls 'the theory of social norms' from a rational choice point of view, extends the attack to the French structuralists and to Pierre Bourdieu.

14. Arguably, many rational choice theorists recognise, like Elias, that the old and vacuous issue of whether 'structure explains action' or 'action explains structure' is a philosophical chicken-and-egg debate, and that people's 'freedom of choice' or feasible sets require theoretical-empirical investigation, not philosophical meditation. As Elias remarks, the old debates overlook the simple fact that 'there are always simultaneously many mutually dependent individuals, whose interdependence to a greater or lesser extent limits each one's scope for action' (1970: 167). Rational choice and games theory clearly embodies this insight, yet the point is blurred by some rational choice theorists' insistence, under the influence of methodological individualist philosophers, that structure, and changes or development in structure, are always ultimately to be explained in terms of action. This can only be true as a truism, and it leads straight back to the old circular debates.

15. Future outcomes are likely to be weighted somewhat less heavily than present ones, according to a 'discount parameter' analogous to the familiar idea of a rate of discount. Chapter 5 of Axelrod's book is devoted to showing how co-operation can emerge *without* foresight in biological systems, but there an evolutionary selection mechanism explicitly substitues for foresight.

16. There are some difficulties in this theory. Elster remarks that it 'does not offer an answer to the crucial question of why people have the aspiration or satisfaction levels they have. . . . These levels must simply be taken as given, which means that the theory offers little more than 'thick description' (1986: 26). This criticism is analogous to the point often made about Darwin's theory of natural selection: it did not actually explain how the random mutation of species came to happen. To those, like sociologists, better content with thick description, the theory seems to fit rather well the results of studies of the internal organisation of firms (see Mennell, 1974: 162–4) and of technical change.

Alchian's line of argument (1950) in effect runs counter to the theory of satisficing behaviour. It amounts to the contention that though maximising strategies may be hit upon by chance or rule of thumb, market forces then select the maximisers and eliminate the submaximisers. Thus it is a theory of rational behaviour, but not of rational choice. Elster (1986: 27) argues that this falls down because—unlike in the world of biological evolution— economic environments change faster than firms adapt, so that an equilibrium state will never be reached, and at any given time there will always be efficient and inefficient firms coexisting in the economy. Effective as this may be against Alchian in the context of the theory of the firm, it does not seem to raise a fundamental problem in the broader context of social development, but does draw further attention to the possibility of the 'survival of the mediocre'.

17. There are exceptions: Olson (1965) discusses how a 'latent group' can become an organised group if free-riding can be overcome.

18. Peter Abell (personal communication) suggests that civilising processes could be seen abstractly as substituting games of 'chicken' for Prisoners' Dilemma games.

19. See the references given in Mennell, 1989a: 241–6.

20. But see Elias's remarks on the period of the upsurge of the *Freikorps*, in his essay 'Civilisation and Violence' (1980).

21. See the excellent recent thesis by Jonathan Fletcher (1988) on Germany in this period.

22. See Elias and Scotson, *The Established and the Outsiders*, 1965; Mennell, 1989a: 115–39.

23. In effect this embodies the stipulation that one must be quite sure, before one speaks of a decivilising process, that civilising trends were dominant for a substantial prior period. Tainter has to propose a parallel criterion when defining what he means by 'collapse'; he treats the passing of the Carolingian Empire not as a case of collapse but merely of unsuccessful empire-building, because it did not sustain its size and complexity for more than two generations (Tainter, 1988: 4).

24. For the fact that they are not in this case, one possible interpretation is that the capacity to react with realistic rather than with neurotic, fantasy-charged, anxiety is itself the outcome of people having undergone a very long civilising process. Thus it may be another instance of people's ability to 'run on their batteries' (see below).

25. The passage illustrates the difficulty of using 'civilisation' in the technical sense Elias wishes to employ; here the translator has used it simply to render the word *Kultur*.

26. Here Weber is perhaps not living up to the highest ideals of *Wertfreiheit*.

Bibliography

Adams, Robert McC. 1966 *The Evolution of Urban Society: Early Mesopotamia and Prehispanic Mexico.* Chicago, Aldine.

Alchian, A.A. 1950 'Uncertainty, Evolution and Economic Theory', *Journal of Political Economy* 58: 211–22.

Anderson, J.L. 1981 'Climatic Change in European Economic History.' *Research in Economic History* 6: 1–34.

Anderson, Perry 1974a *Passages from Antiquity to Feudalism.* London, New Left Books.

—1974b *Lineages of the Absolutist State.* London, New Left Books.

Arrow, Kenneth J. 1951 *Social Choice and Individual Values.* New York, Wiley.

Axelrod, Robert 1984 *The Evolution of Co-operation.* New York: Basic Books.

Azu, Noa Akunor Aguae 1929 *Adangbe (Adangme) History.* Accra, Government Printing Office.

Basu, K., E.L. Jones and E. Schlicht, 1987 'The Growth and Decay of Custom: The Role of the New Institutional Economics in Economic History', *Explorations in Economic History* 24 (1): 1–21.

Bax, Mart 1988 *Religieuze regimes in ontwikkeling: verhulde vormen van macht en afhankelijkheid.* Hilversum, Gooi en Sticht.

Beckerman, W. 1974 *In Defence of Economic Growth.* London, Jonathan Cape.

Bickerman, E.J. 1980 *Chronology of the Ancient World.* 2nd ed. London, Thames and Hudson.

Bielenberg, Christabel [1968] *The Past is Myself.* London, Corgi Books, 1984.

Bloch, Marc 1966 *Land and Work in Medieval Europe.* New York, Harper & Row.

Blumer, Herbert 1969 *Symbolic Interactionism: Perspective and Method.* Englewood Cliffs, N.J., Prentice-Hall.

Boserup, Ester 1965 *The Conditions of Agricultural Growth.* Chicago: Aldine.

—1981 *Population and Technology.* Oxford, Basil Blackwell.

Burke, Peter 1980 *Sociology and History.* London, Allen & Unwin.

Butterfield, Herbert 1981 *The Origins of History.* London, Methuen.

Cairns, E. and Wilson, R. 1985 'Psychiatric Aspects of Violence in Northern Ireland'. *Stress Medicine* 1: 193–201.

Cameron, Rondo 1970 'Europe's Second Logistic', *Comparative Studies in Society and History* 12: 452–62.

Chandler, T., and Fox, G. 1974 *3000 Years of Urban Growth*. New York, Academic Press.

Churchill, Winston S. 1930 *My Early Life*. London, Thornton Butterworth.

Clark, J.D. and J.W.K. Harris 1985 'Fire and its Roles in Early Hominid Lifeways'. *The African Archaeologist* 3: 3–27.

Clark, Stuart 1985 'The *Annales* Historians', in Q. Skinner, ed., *The Return of Grand Theory in the Human Sciences*. Cambridge, Cambridge University Press, pp. 177–98.

Clastres, Pierre 1980 *Recherches d'Anthropologie politique*. Paris, Editions du Seuil.

Clough, S.B. 1961 *The Rise and Fall of Civilization*. New York, Columbia University Press.

Coleman, James S. 1986 *Individual Interests and Collective Action*. Cambridge, Cambridge University Press.

Collins, Randall 1986 *Weberian Sociological Theory*. Cambridge, Cambridge University Press.

Conrad, Geoffrey W. and Arthur A. Demarest 1984 *Religion and Empire: The Dynamics of Aztec and Inca Expansionism*. Cambridge, Cambridge University Press.

Crosby, A.W. 1986 *Ecological Imperialism: The Biological Expansion of Europe, 900–1900*. Cambridge, Cambridge University Press.

Curtin, P.D. 1984 *Cross-cultural Trade in World History*. Cambridge, Cambridge University Press.

Dodgshon, R.A. 1987 *The European Past*. London, Macmillan Education.

Drucker, P. 1987 'Japan's Choices', *Foreign Affairs* 65: 923–941.

Dublin, L.I., Lotka, A.J., and Spiegelman, M. 1936 *Length of Life: A Study of the Life Table*. New York, The Ronald Press.

Duby, Georges 1980 *The Three Orders: Feudal Society Imagined*. Chicago, University of Chicago Press.

Dunning, Eric 1977 'In Defence of Developmental Sociology: A Critique of Popper's *Poverty of Historicism* with special reference to the theory of Auguste Comte'. *Amsterdams Sociologisch Tijdschrift* 4 (3): 327–49.

—1988 'Sport in the Civilising Process'. Inaugural Lecture, University of Leicester. (Publication forthcoming in *Theory, Culture and Society*.)

Dunning, E.G., P. Murphy and J. Williams 1988 *The Roots of Football Hooliganism*. London, Routledge.

Durand, J.D. 1977 'Historical Estimates of World Population: An Evaluation'. *Population and Development Review* 3: 253–296.

Elias, Norbert [1939] *The Civilising Process*. Vol. I, *The History of Manners*, Oxford, Blackwell, 1978; Vol. II, *State Formation and Civilisation* [US: *Power and Civility*], Oxford, Blackwell, 1982.

—[1969] *The Court Society*. Oxford, Blackwell, 1983.

Bibliography 139

—1977 'Zur Grundlegung einer Theorie sozialer Prozess'. *Zeitschrift für Soziologie* 6 (2) 127–49.
—[1970] *What is Sociology?* London, Hutchinson, 1978
—[1980] 'Civilisation and Violence', *Telos* 64, Winter 1982/3: 134–54.
—1984 *Über die Zeit.* Frankfurt, Suhrkamp.
—1985 *Humana Conditio.* Frankfurt, Suhrkamp.
—1987a *Involvement and Detachment.* Oxford, Blackwell.
—1987b 'The Retreat of Sociologists into the Present'. *Theory, Culture and Society* 4 (2–3): 223–48.
—1989 'The Symbol Theory: An Introduction, Part One'. *Theory, Culture and Society* 6 (2): 169–217.
Elias, N. and J. Scotson 1965 *The Established and the Outsiders.* London, Frank Cass.
Elster, Jon 1986 'Introduction' to Elster, ed., *Rational Choice Theory.* Oxford, Basil Blackwell, pp.1–33.
Elvin, Mark 1973 *The Pattern of the Chinese Past.* London, Eyre Methuen.
Finley, M.I. 1977 *The World of Odysseus.* 2nd ed. London, Chatto & Windus.
Fletcher, Jonathan 1988 *On Civilisation, Violence and Decivilising Processes in Germany.* Unpublished MA thesis, University of Essex.
Galloway, P.R. 1986 'Long-term Fluctuations in Climate and Population in the Preindustrial Era', *Population and Development Review* 12: 1–24.
Gellner, Ernest 1988 *Plough, Sword and Book: The Structure of Human History.* London, Collins Harvill.
Gernet, Jacques 1982 *A History of Chinese Civilisation.* Cambridge, Cambridge University Press.
Glassman, Ronald 1986 *Democracy and Despotism in Primitive Societies. A Neo-Weberian Approach.* 2 vols. Millwood, N.Y., Associated Faculty Press.
Glick, T.F. 1979 *Islamic and Christian Spain in the Early Middle Ages.* Princeton, N.J., Princeton University Press.
Goldsmith, R. 1987 *Premodern Financial Systems: A Historical Comparative Study.* Cambridge, Cambridge University Press.
Goldthorpe, John H. 1988 'The Uses of History in Sociology: Reflections on Some Recent Tendencies'. T.H. Marshall Lecture, University of Southampton.
Gottwald, Norman K. 1979 *The Tribes of Yahweh: A Sociology of Liberated Israel 1250–1050 bce* Maryknoll, N.Y., Orbis Books.
Goudsblom, Johan [1960] *Nihilism and Culture.* Oxford: Basil Blackwell 1980.
—1977 *Sociology in the Balance.* Oxford, Basil Blackwell.
—1984 'Die Erforschung von Zivilisationsprozessen'. In P.R. Gleichmann et al, eds., *Macht und Zivilisation.* Frankfurt, Suhrkamp, pp. 129–47.
—1984-88 'Vuur en beschaving'. *De Gids* 147 (1984): 227–43; 148 (1985):

3–27 and 714–22; 149 (1986) 640–52 and 784–802; 151 (1988): 171–88 and 901–11.

—1986 'The Human Monopoly on the Use of Fire: Its Origins and Conditions'. *Human Evolution* 1: 517–23.

—1987 'The Domestication of Fire as a Civilizing Process'. *Theory, Culture and Society* 4 (2–3):457–76.

—1988 'The Impact of the Domestication of Fire upon the Balance of Power Between Human Groups and Other Animals'. Unpublished paper, University of Amsterdam.

—1989 'Stijlen en beschavingen'. *De Gids*, 152: 720–22.

Guha, A.S. 1981 *An Evolutionary View of Economic Growth*. Oxford, Clarendon Press.

Halbwachs, Maurice 1950 *La Mémoire collective*. Paris, Presses Universitaires de France.

Hall, John A. 1985 *Powers and Liberties: The Causes and Consequences of the Rise of the West*. Oxford, Basil Blackwell.

Hallpike, C.R. 1986 *The Principles of Social Evolution*. New York, Oxford University Press.

Harris, Marvin 1968 *The Rise of Anthropological Theory*. New York, Columbia University Press.

—1974 *Cows, Pigs, Wars, and Witches: The Riddle of Culture*. New York, Random House.

—1977 *Cannibals and Kings: The Origins of Cultures*. New York: Random House.

—1985 *Good to Eat: Riddles of Food and Culture*. New York, Simon & Schuster.

—1988 *Culture, People, Nature: An Introduction to General Anthropology*. 5th ed. New York, Harper & Row.

Harris, Marvin and Eric B. Ross 1987 *Death, Sex, and Fertility: Population Regulation in Preindustrial and Developing Societies*. New York, Columbia University Press 1987.

Hindess, Barry 1988 *Choice, Rationality and Social Theory*. London, Unwin Hyman.

Hirschman, A.O. 1985 *A Bias for Hope*. Boulder and London, Westview Encore.

Hopkins, Keith 1978 *Conquerors and Slaves: Sociological Studies in Roman Society*. Vol. I, Cambridge, Cambridge University Press.

Hosin, A.A. 1983 *The Impact of International Conflict on Children's and Adoloscents's National Perceptions*. Unpublished PhD thesis, University of Ulster.

Huber, Hugo 1963 *The Krobo: Traditional Social and Religious Life of a West African People*. St. Augustin near Bonn, Anthropos Institute.

Ingold, Tim 1986 *Evolution and Social Life*. Cambridge, Cambridge University Press.

Jackson, R.H. 1987 'Quasi-states, dual regimes, and neoclassical theory: International jurisprudence and the Third World', *International Organization* 41: 519-549.

Jacobsen, Thorkild 1939 *The Sumerian King List*. Chicago, University of Chicago Press.

James, Steven R. 1989 'Hominid Use of Fire in the Lower and Middle Pleistocene', *Current Anthroplogy* 30: 1-26.

Johnson, Allen W. and Timothy Earle 1987 *The Evolution of Human Societies: From Foraging Group to Agrarian State*. Stanford, Stanford University Press.

Jones, E.L. [1981] *The European Miracle: Environments, Economies, and Geopolitics in the History of Europe and Asia*. 2nd ed. Cambridge, Cambridge University Press 1987.

—1982 'No Stationary State: The World before Industrialisation', Workshop in Economic History, Department of Economics, University of Chicago, 8283-9.

—1985 *Very Long-Term Economic Development as the History Survey*. *Economics Discussion Papers*, No. 2/85. Bundoora, School of Economics, La Trobe University.

—1988 *Growth Recurring: Economic Change in World History*. Oxford, Clarendon Press.

—1989a 'A New Political History of Economic Growth'. *Policy*, forthcoming.

—1989b Review of J.A. Tainter, *The Collapse of Complex Societies*, *Economic History Review* (forthcoming)

Jones, S.R.H. 1988 'Economic Growth and the Spread of the Market Principle in Later Anglo-Saxon England', *University of Auckland Working Papers in Economics* No. 48.

Kaufmann, Walter (ed.) 1968 *Basic Writings of Nietzsche*. New York, Random House.

Keene, D. 1969 *The Japanese Discovery of Europe: Honda Toshiaki and other Discoveries 1720-1798*. Stanford, Stanford University Press.

Keynes, John Maynard 1951 *Essays in Persuasion*. London, Rupert Hart-Davis.

Konvitz, Josef W., ed. 1985 *What Americans Should Know: Western Civilisation or World History?* Lansing, Michigan State University Press.

Kuhn, Thomas S. 1970 *The Structure of Scientific Revolutions*. 2nd ed. Chicago: University of Chicago Press.

Kunio, Y. 1986 *Japanese Economic Development*. Tokyo, Oxford University Press.

Kuran, T. 1988 'The Tenacious Past: Theories of Personal and Collective Conservatism', *Journal of Economic Behavior and Organization* 10: 143-171.

Ladurie, E. Le Roy 1973 'L'Unification microbienne du monde', *Revue Suisse d'histoire*, 673–692.

Langer, Herbert 1981 *The Thirty Years War*. Poole, Blandford Press.

Leach, Sir Edmund 1986 'Violence'. *London Review of Books*, 23 October.

Lenski, Gerhard 1966 *Power and Privilege: A Theory of Social Stratification*. New York, McGraw-Hill.

Levi, Primo 1987 *Moments of Reprieve*. London, Sphere Books.

Lewis, W.Arthur 1955 *The Theory of Economic Growth*. London, George Allen and Unwin.

Lincoln, Bruce 1981 *Priests, Warriors and Cattle: A Study in the Ecology of Religions*. Berkeley, University of California Press.

Lloyd, Seton 1984 *The Archaeology of Mesopotamia*. 2nd ed. London, Thames and Hudson.

Luce, R.D. and H. Raiffa 1957 *Games and Decisions*. New York, Wiley.

McCormack, G. 1988 'Japan's Superpower Dilemmas', University of Adelaide Centre for Asian Studies Public Lecture Series, *Understanding Japan*, 3–13.

MacDonald, Michael D. 1983 *Children of Wrath: Political Violence in Northern Ireland*. Unpublished PhD thesis, University of California, Berkeley.

McEvedy, C. and Jones, R. 1978 *Atlas of World Population History*. Harmondsworth, Penguin Books.

Mackenzie, W.J.M. 1978 *Biological Ideas in Politics*. Harmondsworth, Penguin Books.

MacMullen, Ramsay 1974 *Roman Social Relations, 50 BC to AD 284*. New Haven, Yale University Press.

McNeill, William H. 1963 *The Rise of the West: A History of the Human Community*. Chicago, University of Chicago Press.

—[1976] *Plagues and Peoples*. Harmondsworth, Penguin, 1979.

—1982 *The Pursuit of Power*. Chicago, University of Chicago Press.

—1984 'Human Migration in Historical Perspective'. *Population and Development Review* 10: 1–18.

—1986 *Mythistory and Other Essays*. Chicago, University of Chicago Press.

Maddison, A. 1982 *Phases of Capitalist Development*. Oxford, Oxford University Press.

Maine, Sir Henry 1883 *Dissertations on Early Law and Custom*. London, John Murray.

Mann, Michael 1986 *The Sources of Social Power*. Vol. 1. *A History of Power from the Beginning to AD 1760*. Cambridge, Cambridge University Press.

March, James G. [1978] 'Bounded Rationality, Ambiguity and the Engineering of Choice', reprinted in Jon Elster, ed. *Rational Choice Theory*. Oxford. Basil Blackwell, pp.142–170.

Maso, Benjo 1982 'Riddereer en riddermoed—ontwikkelingen van de aanvalslust in de late middeleeuwen'. *Sociologische Gids* 29 (3–4): 296–325.
Mayhew, Anne 1987 'Culture: Core Concept under Attack', *Journal of Economic Issues* 21: 587–603.
Menken, J. and Watkins, S. Cotts 1985 'Famines in Historical Perspective', *Population and Development Review* 11: 647–675.
Mennell, Stephen 1974 *Sociological Theory: Uses and Unities*. London, Thomas Nelson.
—1989a *Norbert Elias: Civilisation and the Human Self-Image*. Oxford, Basil Blackwell.
—1989b 'The Sociological Study of History: Institutions and Social Development', in C.G.A. Bryant and H. Becker, eds., *What has Sociology Achieved?*. London, Macmillan.
Nelson, R. and S. Winter 1982 *An Evolutionary Theory of Economic Change*. Cambridge, Mass., Harvard University Press.
von Neumann J. and O. Morgenstern 1944 *Theory of Games and Economic Behaviour*. Princeton, NJ, Princeton University Press.
Nisbet, Robert A. 1969 *Social Change and History*. New York: Oxford University Press.
Noakes, J. and G. Pridham, eds. 1988 *Nazism 1919–1945*. Vol. III, *Foreign Policy, War and Racial Extermination*. Exeter, University of Exeter.
Oliver, P.E. and G. Marwell 1988 'The Paradox of Group Size in Collective Action'. *American Sociological Review*, 53 (1): 1–8.
Olson, Mancur Jr. 1965 *The Logic of Collective Action*. Cambridge, Mass., Harvard University Press.
Past Worlds: The Times Atlas of Archaeology 1988. London, Times Books.
Patel, S.J. 1964 'The Economic Distance between Nations: Its Origin, Measurement and Outlook', *Economic Journal* LXXIV: 119–131.
Perlès, Catherine 1987 'La naissance du feu'. *L'Histoire* 105 (December): 28–33.
Persson, K.G. 1988 *Pre-industrial Economic Growth*. Oxford, Basil Blackwell.
Popper, Karl R. 1945 *The Open Society and its Enemies*. 2 vols., London, Routledge and Kegan Paul.
—1957 *The Poverty of Historicism*. London, Routledge and Kegan Paul.
Rapoport, Anatol 1960 *Fights, Games and Debates*. Ann Arbor, University of Michigan Press.
Reid, A. 1988 *Southeast Asia in the Age of Commerce 1450-1680*. Vol. 1: *The Lands below the Winds*. New Haven, Yale University Press.
Rozman, G. 1973 *Urban Networks in Ch'ing China and Tokugawa Japan*. Princeton, Princeton University Press.
Rüstow, Alexander 1950 *Ortsbestimmung der Gegenwart. Eine universalgeschichtliche Kulturkritik*. Vol. 1. *Ursprung der Herrschaft*. Zürich: Eugen Rentsch.

Sagarra, Eda 1977 *A Social History of Germany, 1648–1914*. London, Methuen.

Sahlins, Marshall 1972 *Stone Age Economics*. Chicago, Aldine.

Sanderson, Stephen K. 1989 'Evolutionism without Developmentalism: Two Models of Explanation in Theories of Social Evolution". Paper presented at American Sociological Association Annual Meeting, San Francisco, 12 August 1989.

—1990 *Social Evolutionism: A Critical History*. Cambridge, Mass., Basil Blackwell (forthcoming).

Schotter, M. 1981 *The Economic Theory of Social Institutions*. Cambridge, Cambridge University Press.

Simon, Herbert A. 1957 *Models of Man*. New York, Wiley.

Singh, R.C.P. 1968 *Kingship in Northern India (cir. 600 AD–1200 AD)*. Delhi, Motilal Banarsidass.

Sitwell, N.H.H. 1986 *Outside the Empire: The World the Romans Knew*. London, Paladin.

Smith, C.S. 1981 *A Search for Structure*. Cambridge, Mass., MIT Press.

Spencer, Herbert 1862 *First Principles*. New York, Appleton.

Stone, J. and Mennell, S.J., eds., 1980 *Alexis de Tocqueville on Democracy, Revolution and Society*. Chicago, University of Chicago Press.

Stover, Leon E. and Takeko Kawai Stover 1977 *China: An Anthropological Perspective*. Pacific Palisades, Cal., Goodyear.

de Swaan, Abram 1988 *In Care of the State: Health Care, Education and Welfare in Europe and the USA in the Modern Era*. Cambridge, Polity Press.

Taagepera, Rein 1978 'Size and Duration of Empires: systematics of size'. *Social Science Research* 7: 108–27.

Taagepera, Rein, and Colby, B.N. 1979 'Growth of Western Civilisation: Epicyclical or Exponential?' *American Anthropologist* 81: 907–912.

Tainter, Joseph A. 1988 *The Collapse of Complex Societies*. Cambridge, Cambridge University Press.

Taylor, Charles, 1971 'Interpretation and the Sciences of Man', *Review of Metaphysics* 25: 3–51.

Tylecote, R.F. 1987 *The Early History of Metallurgy in Europe*. London, Longman.

Tylor, Edward B. 1871 *Primitive Culture*. Vol. 1. *The Origins of Culture*. Gloucester, Mass., Smith.

Ullmann-Margalit, Edna 1978 *The Emergence of Norms*. Oxford, Clarendon Press.

Usher, D. 1973 'An imputation to the measure of economic growth for changes in life expectancy', in M. Moss, ed., *The Measurement of Economic and Social Performance*. Conference in Income and Wealth, Vol. 38, New York, National Bureau of Economic Research.

de Vries, J. 1984 *European Urbanization 1500–1800*. Cambridge, Mass., Harvard University Press.

Wallace, A.R. 1962 *The Malay Archipelago*. New York, Dover.

Wallerstein, Immanuel 1974 *The Modern World-System*, Vol. I. New York, Academic Press.

Weber, Max [1896] 'The Social Causes of the Decline of Ancient Civilisation', in *The Agrarian Sociology of Ancient Civilisations*. London, New Left Books, 1976, pp. 389–411

—[1904–5] *The Protestant Ethic and the Spirit of Capitalism*. London, Allen and Unwin, 1930.

—[1922] *Economy and Society*. 2 vols. New York, Bedminster 1968.

Wenke, Robert J. 1984 *Past Worlds: Humankind's First Three Million Years*. 2nd ed. New York, Oxford University Press.

West, M.L. 1978 *Hesiod: Works and Days*. Oxford, Clarendon Press.

Wichers, A.J. 1965 *De Oude Plattelandsbeschaving: Een Sociologische Bewustwording van de Overherigheid*. Assen, Van Gorcum.

Wilson, Bryan 1975 *The Noble Savages: The Primitive Origins of Charisma and its Contemporary Survival*. Berkeley, University of California Press.

Wittfogel, Karl A. [1957] *Oriental Despotism: A Comparative Study of Total Power*. 2nd ed. New York, Random House 1981.

Wolf, Eric R. 1959 *Sons of the Shaking Earth. The People of Mexico and Guatemala*. Chicago, University of Chicago Press.

—1982 *Europe and the People Without History*. Berkeley, University of California Press.

Wrong, Dennis H. 1961 'The Oversocialised Conception of Man in Modern Sociology'. *American Sociological Review* 26 (2): 183–93.

Index

Biographical Notes

Johan Goudsblom is Professor of Sociology at the University of Amsterdam. He studied at Wesleyan University, Middletown, Conn., and the University of Amsterdam. He has been a Visiting Fellow at Princeton and Berkeley and a Visiting Professor at Konstanz and Exeter. His publications in English include *Dutch Society* (Random House, 1967), *Sociology in the Balance* (Basil Blackwell, 1977), and *Nihilism and Culture* (Basil Blackwell, 1980). His two most recent books in Dutch are collections of essays on the sociology of Norbert Elias (1987) and on language and social reality (1988). His current research is focused on the domestication of fire as a long-term socio-cultural process.

Eric Jones is a Professor in the School of Economics at La Trobe University, Melbourne, Australia, and Visiting Professor of Economic History at the University of Exeter. He has also taught at Oxford, Reading, Northwestern, Purdue and Yale, and been a Member of the Institute for Advanced Study at Princeton. He is a member of the Comparative Economic History group at La Trobe and has published two books on very long-term change in large systems, *The European Miracle* (Cambridge University Press, 1981, 2nd ed. 1987) and *Growth Recurring* (Oxford University Press, 1988).

Stephen Mennell is Reader in Sociology and Comparative European Studies at the University of Exeter. He read economics at Cambridge and has been Frank Knox Fellow in the Department of Social Relations at Harvard and a Fellow of the Netherlands Institute for Advanced Study, Wassenaar. His two most recent books are *All Manners of Food* (Basil Blackwell, 1985) and *Norbert Elias: Civilisation and the Human Self-Image* (Basil Blackwell, 1989).